Fabulous
Québec City

Experience the Passion of **Québec City**!

Ulysses Travel Guides

Associate Editors
Annie Gilbert, Marie-Josée Guy, Pierre Ledoux

Artistic Director
Pascal Biet

Page Layout
Philippe Thomas

Cover Page Layout
Marie-France Denis

Iconographic Research
Nadège Picard

Cartographer
Kirill Berdnikov

Copy Editing
Matthew McLauchlin

Research, Writing and Translation (Extracts From Ulysses Guide *Québec City*)
Marie-Josée Béliveau, Cindy Garayt, Isabel Gosselin, Marie-Josée Guy, Janet Logan, Stéphane G. Marceau, Matthew McLauchlin, François Rémillard, Alain Rondeau, Christopher Woodward

Cover Page Photo
Château Frontenac at night: ©Alexandre Payette

This work was produced under the direction of Olivier Gougeon.

Acknowledgements
Ulysses Travel Guides would like to give special thanks to Jérôme Bégin and Nicolas Tremblay, Services des archives de la Ville de Québec; Marie-Claude Belley, Parks Canada; Agnès Dufour, Musée de la civilisation; Jean-Claude Germain; Marielle Lavertu, Bibliothèque et Archives Nationales du Québec; Philippe Renault.

Kristin C. Anderson; Éric Bealieu; Andrew Belding; John Bennett; Étienne Boucher; David Brisebois; Louis Carrier; Annie Caya; Gaétane Chabot, Parc maritime du Saint-Laurent; Lucie Cloutier, Grand Théâtre de Québec; Marie-France Côté, Roy et Turner Communications; Nataly Deschamps, Canyon Sainte-Anne; Hélène Dupont, Sépaq; Igor Geiller; Marie-Ève Guérard, Université de Laval; Jonathan Habel; David Paul Ohmer; Jonathan Houle; Hélène Huard; Chantal Javaux, Manoir Mauvide-Genest; Jeff Hawkins; Lynn Lafontaine, Library and Archives Canada; Yves Laframboise; Lucie Laplante, Conseil des monuments et sites du Québec; Fernand Larochelle; Annie Latour, Maison Drouin; Chantal Lepire, Réserve nationale de faune du cap Tourmente; Joyce Li; Samantha McKinley, Mont-Sainte-Anne/Stoneham; Michèle Moffet, Carnaval de Québec; Alexandre Payette; Hélène Pineault, Société du Centre des Congrès de Québec; Mariette Provencher; Marie-Claude Ravary, Conseil du patrimoine religieux du Québec; Marie-Hélène Raymond, Daniel Roberge, Société du domaine Maizerets; Phyllis Smith, Musée national des beaux-arts du Québec; Roxanne Saint-Pierre, Société du 400ᵉ anniversaire de Québec; Véronique Saint-Jacques, Ex Machina; Eliza Tasbihi.

We acknowledge the financial support of the Government of Canada through the Book Publishing Industry Development Program (BPIDP) for our publishing activities. We would also like to thank the Government of Québec – Tax credit for book publishing – Administered by SODEC.

Bibliothèque et Archives nationales du Québec and Library and Archives Canada cataloguing in publication

Main entry under title :

Fabulous Québec City : experience the passion of Québec!

(Fabulous)
Translation of: Fabuleuse Québec.
Includes index.

ISBN 978-2-89464-893-3

1. Québec (Québec) - Guidebooks. 2. Québec (Québec) - Pictorial works. I. Series.

FC2946.18.F3213 2009   917.14'471045   C2008-942311-9

▶ A fanciful facade in the Petit-Champlain neighbourhood. ©Jean-Claude Germain

© Rachid Lamzah

Contents

List of Maps

Map Symbols

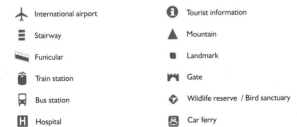

International airport

Stairway

Funicular

Train station

Bus station

Hospital

Tourist information

Mountain

Landmark

Gate

Wildlife reserve / Bird sanctuary

Car ferry

Rich in history and architecture, magnificent Québec City is set amidst an exceptional natural landscape. Even though Québec City is one of the oldest cities in North America and the oldest in Canada, it is firmly turned to the future. The Haute-Ville (upper town) sits on a promontory, Cap Diamant, which is more than 98m high and juts out over the St. Lawrence River. During his third trip, Jacques Cartier called this rocky outcrop "Cap aux Diamants," believing he had discovered diamonds and gold here. But he quickly learned that these precious stones were nothing more than common fool's gold and quartz. Nevertheless, Cap Diamant became the future site of Québec City when Samuel de Champlain established a fur trading post and fortified buildings, creating the settlement known as the "Abitation."

This location played a strategic role in New France's defence system. Here the St. Lawrence River is only 1km wide, and it is this narrowing of the river that gave Québec City the name "Kebec," an Algonquin word meaning "place where the river narrows." Perched on top of Cap Diamant and surrounded by major fortifications from very early on, the city is commonly dubbed the "Gibraltar of North America."

This fortification did not succeed, however, in driving back the English troops who finally captured the city at the Battle of the Plains of Abraham. Yet the French colony managed to retain its cultural identity after the Conquest. Well protected inside its walls, Québec City's heart continued to beat, making it the centre of French Canadian culture in North America.

In 1985, in order to preserve and promote Québec City and its cultural treasures, UNESCO declared the city's historic area—the only walled city in North America north of Mexico—the continent's first World Heritage Site.

Affectionately known as the "Vieille Capitale" (Old Capital), but usually simply called "Québec" by the Québécois, Québec City is the soul of the French-speaking Americas. Thousands of tourists visit it every year and marvel at the city's many charms, its European atmosphere and its inhabitants' *joie de vivre* and hospitality. The architecture and narrow cobblestone streets give the city its character. A romantic place that never fails to fascinate, Québec City has been a source of inspiration to artists for more than three centuries. It is a delight for both the eye and the soul. This little gem is irresistible and whether you visit in the summer, winter, spring or autumn, you cannot help but give in to its charm.

◀ View of the Place d'Armes in 1832. © [1832]. AVQ/ Sproule, R.A./ N016709

▲ Québec City, the "Gibraltar of America". ©[1840]. AVQ/ Bartlett, Chas W., dessinateur Wallis, R./N008393

GEOGRAPHY

Québec City covers an area of 450km² and has a population of more than half a million people, mostly French-speaking. Its eight boroughs—La Cité, Les Rivières, Sainte-Foy–Sillery, Charlesbourg, Beauport, Limoilou, La Haute-Saint-Charles, and Laurentien—are each divided into a patchwork of different neighbourhoods.

Downtown Québec City occupies the Saint-Roch neighbourhood in the Basse-Ville area. The Haute-Ville (upper town) and Basse-Ville (lower town) are an easy geographical reference commonly used by the city's residents. You'll have no trouble telling the first, with its prosperous buildings atop Cap Diamant, from the second, an area with working-class roots spreading from the foot of the cape.

Geography

HISTORY

The First Europeans

The first Europeans to reach the coast of North America were the Vikings, who explored the region in the 10th century. They were followed by whalers and fishers in search of cod. However, beginning in 1534, Jacques Cartier made three journeys that marked a turning point in this segment of North American history and were the first official contacts between France and the New World. Cartier's mission for the king of France, François I, was to discover a passage to the East and find the gold and other riches that France needed so badly at the time. After Cartier's failure to fulfill his mission, France abandoned these new lands, considering them unimportant.

A few decades later, the considerable profit that could be made in the fur trade rekindled French interest in New France. In 1608, Samuel de Champlain chose the site where Québec City is now located to set up the first permanent trading post. Champlain was surprised not to find the Aboriginal people that Cartier had described following his journeys. During this time, the sedentary Iroquois who farmed and hunted had moved south and were replaced by the nomadic Algonquins who subsisted on hunting and gathering. The Algonquins became France's main allies. Unlike the Iroquois, they did not have a very strong sense of land ownership and did not show any resistance when the French settled on their territory. The Algonquins agreed to take part in the fur trade with the French.

▼ Champlain's arrival in Québec, 1608. ©Library and Archives Canada/C-01101 5k

IMPORTANT DATES IN QUÉBEC CITY'S HISTORY

1525: Basque fishermen range up the St. Lawrence River and around the Rivière Saguenay.

1535: Jacques Cartier reaches the mouth of the Rivière Sainte-Croix (today called Rivière Saint-Charles), near the Iroquois village of Stadaconé. He is welcomed by Donnacona, the village chief.

1608: On July 3, Samuel de Champlain founds a fur trading post on the Native site called "Kébec," under the governorship of Pierre Dugua, Sieur de Mons, who holds a trade monopoly. He has an "Abitation" built here.

1615: The Récollets arrive in Québec City.

▲ Imaginary portrait of Jacques Cartier.
©Library and Archives Canada/C-011226

1617: The Parisian apothecary Louis Hébert moves to Québec City, becoming the first true colonist in New France.

1625: The Jesuits arrive in Québec City.

1627-1663: The Compagnie des Cent-Associés becomes responsible for populating the colony. The company's chief shareholders include such figures as Samuel de Champlain and Cardinal de Richelieu.

1629: Québec City is captured for England by the Kirke brothers; the Récollets are expelled.

1632: The treaty of Saint-Germain-en-Laye returns New France to French control.

1639: The Ursuline nuns and Marie de l'Incarnation (Marie Guyart) arrive in Québec City to teach young girls.

1659: Monseigneur François de Laval arrives to serve as the first bishop of New France.

1663: Québec City becomes the capital of New France. Some 550 people now live in Québec City, with a further 1,400 colonists living in the hinterlands.

1665: Jean Talon arrives and takes office as Intendant of New France.

1670: The Récollets return to New France.

1672-1682: First mandate of Louis de Buade, Comte de Frontenac et de Palluau, as governor of New France.

1686: Place Royale is created in Québec City and a bust of King Louis XIV is installed.

1689-1698: Second mandate of Frontenac as governor of New France.

1690: Facing Québec City with his fleet, English Admiral William Phips orders the French to surrender. Governor Frontenac responds to Phips' emissary with the famous words, "I will not make you wait so long. No, I will not answer your general but with the mouths of my cannons and with gunfire; let him learn that this is not the way to address a man like me. Let him do his best, as I will do mine." He succeeds in repelling the English assault.

1711: Part of the fleet of British Admiral Hovenden Walker, on its way to attack Québec City, is shipwrecked by bad weather north of Île d'Anticosti on the reefs of Île aux Œufs. Walker retreats.

1737: The Chemin du Roy is opened between Montréal and Québec.

▼   Cap Diamant in 1832. ©Library and Archives Canada/C-040013k

1756: Start of the Seven Years' War between France and Great Britain, as well as between Austria and Prussia.

1759: On 13 September, British troops under General James Wolfe land at Anse au Foulon and scale Cap Diamant, ambushing the French troops under General Montcalm and defeating them in the brief Battle of the Plains of Abraham.

1763: The Treaty of Paris ends the Seven Years' War; among other provisions, it cedes New France to Great Britain.

1763-1791: following the British Conquest, the former capital of New France becomes the capital of the Province of Quebec.

1775: The American army invades Québec City. The American commander Richard Montgomery and much of the American force are killed in battle.

1791: The *Constitutional Act* of 1791 divides Canada into two parts: Lower Canada (now southern Québec) and Upper Canada (now southern Ontario).

1791-1841: Québec City serves as the capital of the colony of Lower Canada.

1792: Québec City is incorporated by royal proclamation.

1820-1830: The Citadelle is built to plans by Elias Walker Durnford.

1832: The legislature of Lower Canada votes to charter the *Cité de Québec*.

1837-1838: The Patriotes Revolt.

1840: Upper and Lower Canada are merged into the Province of Canada.

1844: Québec City's first French bookstore is opened by the Crémazie brothers.

1845: Fires ravage the neighbourhoods of Saint-Roch and Saint-Jean.

1852: Université Laval is founded in Québec City.

1852-1856 and 1859-1866: Québec City is the capital of Canada.

1854: The seigneurial system is abolished.

1857: Ottawa obtains the title of capital of Canada; the government moves there in 1866.

1866: Second fire in the Saint-Roch district.

1867: Birth of the Canadian Confederation. The province of Québec is created with Québec City as capital.

1870: Third fire in the Saint-Roch district.

1877-1886: Construction of the Hôtel du Parlement (Québec National Assembly building) to the plans of Eugène-Étienne Taché.

1877-1896: Construction of the Hôtel de Ville (city hall).

1881: Faubourg Saint-Jean and Faubourg Saint-Louis burn to the ground.

1892: Construction of the Château Frontenac begins, to the plans of American architect Bruce Price.

1896: The newspaper *Le Soleil*, offspring of *L'Électeur*, begins publication. The official journal of the Liberal Party of Canada and the Québec Liberal Party, *L'Électeur* had counted Canadian prime minister Wilfrid Laurier and Québec premier Honoré Mercier among its founders.

1899: The Saint-Roch neighbourhood again burns down.

1907: The Pont de Québec collapses during construction.

1916: The Pont de Québec collapses a second time during construction.

1918: Anti-conscription riots break out. The army fires on the crowd, killing four in the Saint-Sauveur neighbourhood.

▲ Construction of the Pont de Québec, early 20th century. ©[1917?]. AVQ, N011422

1919: The Pont de Québec, the world's longest cantilever bridge, is officially opened. The bridge crosses the St. Lawrence, linking Québec City on the north bank to Lévis on the south by train.

1929: Inauguration of the road crossing on the Pont de Québec.

1932: Inauguration of the Palais Montcalm in Québec City.

1943 and 1944: During the Second World War, Québec City hosts two conferences of the Allies at the Château Frontenac and the Citadelle. The 1943 conference brings together US President Franklin Delano Roosevelt, British Prime Minister Winston Churchill, Canadian Prime Minister William Lyon Mackenzie King, and Chinese foreign affairs minister T.V. Soong. Churchill and Roosevelt return for the 1944 conference.

1957: The Aéroport de Québec is opened in L'Ancienne-Lorette.

1963: A monument to Queen Victoria is bombed with dynamite.

1964: Queen Elizabeth II, Queen of Canada, visits Québec City. A demonstration is violently put down by the police, an event known as "Samedi de la Matraque" (Truncheon Saturday).

1966: The Dow brewery closes its Québec City factory after 16 people die from drinking its beer.

1971: Inauguration of the Grand Théâtre de Québec.

1984: Corporal Denis Lortie kills three people at the National Assembly.

1985: Vieux-Québec, Québec City's historic district, is named a World Heritage Site by UNESCO, North America's first.

1988: Inauguration of the Musée de la Civilisation in Québec City.

1995: Québec City loses its hockey team, the Québec Nordiques, to the U.S. state of Colorado. Ironically, the Colorado Avalanche win the Stanley Cup that same year.

2000: The National Assembly passes a law to merge numerous municipalities in Québec.

2001: Québec City hosts the third Summit of the Americas, whose goal is to create the Free Trade Area of the Americas (FTAA). The event is most remembered for the large security barrier around the conference site and clashes between police and anti-globalization protesters.

2002: The new, merged city of Québec, divided into eight boroughs, is established on January 1.

2006: After 75 years, the Jardin Zoologique du Québec, Canada's oldest zoo, closes.

2007: The Fontaine de Tourny is inaugurated in front of the National Assembly, a 400th birthday gift to Québec City from the Simons family, owner of the department store chain.

2008: Québec City celebrates its 400th anniversary with a lavish year-long series of festivities.

▼ A sea of Québec flags during the Fête Nationale. ©*Comité de la fête nationale*

▲ The Québec "Abitation" built under Champlain. ©[1880]. AVQ, N009827

To understand Québec City's place in history, one must appreciate all the advantages of its location. Perched atop Cap Diamant, the city occupies a strategic location overlooking what at the time was the only waterway leading to the North American interior. When Samuel de Champlain decided to establish the first permanent fur-trading outpost and built a fort around the few existing buildings here, it was primarily because of Cap Diamant's strategic advantages. Here, the river narrows considerably and it is easy to block passing ships. Champlain had a wooden fortress built here, which he named the "Abitation." It enclosed the trading post and the homes of various fur traders.

During that first harsh winter in Québec City, 20 of the 28 men that were posted there died of scurvy or malnutrition before ships carrying fresh supplies arrived in the spring of 1609. When Samuel de Champlain died on Christmas Day, 1635, there were about 300 pioneers living in New France.

Between 1627 and 1663, the Compagnie des Cent-Associés held a monopoly on the fur trade and ensured the slow growth of the colony. Meanwhile, French religious orders became more and more interested in New France. The Récollets arrived first, in 1615; they were later replaced by the Jesuits, who began arriving in 1632.

History

The 17th Century

Despite the presence of major tributaries nearby—water being the only efficient means of transport and communication at the time—Québec City was never able to profit as much from the fur trade as Montréal or Trois-Rivières. Throughout the 17th century, merchants, farmers and craftspeople came to settle in Québec City and its surrounding region. The city's economy diversified, namely thanks to its port (which became one of the busiest in the world), its shipbuilding yard and its lumber, which was exported mainly to France. The fur trade, however, remained the leading area of economic activity up until the beginning of the 19th century.

During the 17th century, Québec City became one of the most important centres of commerce in the New World. It was the apex of an economic triangle formed by Acadia, New France and Louisiana, and would become the seat of French power in the Americas. Also, since religious institutions and political powers looked for protection inside the walls of the Haute-Ville, Québec City quickly became the political, administrative and military centre of New France.

Many colonists settled in Québec City. The Basse-Ville (lower town) developed rapidly, expanding to the point where it was necessary to fill in parts of the St. Lawrence River to gain more land. At this time, the risk of fire was great because of the densely packed buildings and the use of wood as the main construction material. In August 1682, flames devastated the Basse-Ville, and the city was later rebuilt according to new standards requiring the use of stone instead of wood for building construction.

RUE DES PAINS-BÉNITS

If you visit the city during the holidays, consider visiting Place Royale, especially on January 3. This is the feast day of Saint Geneviève, patron of Paris, which is celebrated at Église Notre-Dame-des-Victoires where a chapel and altar were dedicated to the saint in 1724.

On this day, blessed bread rolls are distributed to the people. Tradition holds that the little rolls are especially good luck for mothers and the unemployed. During the siege of Paris by the Franks, the courageous saint is said to have given out bread to feed the besieged citizens, and today is invoked against famine. The little street that runs along the east side of the church is called Rue des Pains-Bénits (blessed bread street). As you eat your bread, take a look at the nativity scene inside the church.

Unfortunately, many inhabitants did not have the money to abide by these new requirements and were forced to build outside the city walls, creating the first suburbs. Most of the stone houses in Vieux-Québec today date from this period.

The French-British Rivalry

The economic and strategic importance of Québec City made it a choice target very early on and the capital of New France had to defend itself against a covetous England. The conflicts between France and England had repercussions on the North American colonies, even though the various declarations of war and peace treaties were the result of European politics and had nothing to do with the affairs of the colonies. Consequently, the citadel fell in 1629 when it was attacked by British forces led by the Kirke brothers, but it was quickly returned to France in 1632.

During the 18th century, the French-English rivalry increased as their colonies developed. The ever increasing pressure of British forces in New France finally resulted in the Battle of the Plains of Abraham, part of the Seven Years' War. Arriving near Québec City in July 1759, General Wolfe's troops captured the town on September 13 of the same year, before reinforcements could arrive from France. During the night, the English climbed Cap Diamant to the west of the fortified walls and in the morning, to the great surprise of the French, they were on the Plains of Abraham. The battle began and ended a short time later with the defeat of the Marquis de Montcalm's troops at the hands of General Wolfe; neither general survived.

▼ Québec City under the British Regime. ©[ca 1772]. AVQ, N010869

MONTCALM'S FINAL RESTING PLACE, 242 YEARS AFTER HIS DEATH

During the Battle of the Plains of Abraham, which pitted France against Britain on September 13, 1759, the French troops of General Louis-Joseph de Saint-Véran, Marquis de Montcalm, were defeated by the British forces of General Wolfe. New France was lost to the British.

▼ Portrait of British General James Wolfe.
©Library and Archives Canada/C-003916k

▼ The Marquis de Montcalm leading his troops in the Battle of the Plains of Abraham.
©Library and Archives Canada/C-073720k

Montcalm died the next day of his injuries, and was buried in the chapel of the Ursulines on Rue Donnacona within the city walls. In 2001, 242 years later, the Government of Québec decided to transfer his body to the cemetery of the Hôpital Général, which holds the remains of the numerous soldiers whom the Augustine nuns tried in vain to save.

On October 11, 2001, the representatives of the government accompanied the funeral procession from the chapel to the cemetery, where a mausoleum to Montcalm had been erected. The entrance to the mausoleum is marked with Montcalm's name and coat of arms, as well as a commemorative plaque. A memorial to the Seven Years' War was also erected in the cemetery on that occasion, honouring the soldiers who fell during the war from 1756 to 1763. The sculpture *Traversée sans retour* by Pascale Archambault dominates the memorial.

The cemetery of the Hôpital Général is located in the Saint-Roch neighbourhood, near the edge of the Saint-Sauveur neighbourhood. Located away from downtown in a bend of the Rivière Saint-Charles, this "memorial park" is open to those who wish to visit and reflect.

The British Regime

The Treaty of Paris, signed on February 10, 1763, sealed the French defeat by officially giving New France to the British, marking the end of the French colony in Canada. Under the British Regime, Québec City was transformed. For French Canadians, the Conquest meant that they were now under British rule and ties between the colony and France were cut off, leaving Québec an orphan.

Significant changes occurred as the English replaced the francophones in political and administrative positions. Many of New France's well-to-do inhabitants decided to return to France at the suggestion of the British government. However, most residents and small merchants could not afford the journey and had no choice but to remain in the British colony. The summit of Cap Diamant was also where the English set up their government, which now had the task of managing a considerable portion of North America.

Like the rest of the colony, Québec City was able to resist British assimilation thanks to the Catholic Church and very limited anglophone immigration. Sheltered behind its walls, Québec City remained almost completely francophone for a long time.

However, the situation changed rapidly when the American War of Independence came to an end and the Loyalists, faithful to the British Crown, left the United States to settle on British soil. Many of these new arrivals chose Québec City and Montréal, radically changing the look of the capital, which saw its anglophone population grow considerably.

In addition to Loyalist immigration, many immigrants arrived from the British Isles to settle in Québec City and work in factories or as stevedores in the port. Among them were a significant number of Irish immigrants, who had an important common trait with the local population: the Catholic religion. Anglophones represented approximately 40% of the population in the Québec City region, which at that time was enjoying significant economic growth. This great anglophone immigration, however, was offset by a large influx of francophones from rural Québec.

The 19th Century

The beginning of the 19th century was marked by a period of prosperity, primarily as a result of Napoleon's maritime embargo against Britain, which caused a great lack of raw materials. This demand made Québec City an important trade link between the colony, the West Indies and Britain, and went so far as to make Québec City the third busiest port in North America after New York and New Orleans.

Québec City's port and the various shipyards set up under the French Regime continued to develop until the invention of iron hulls and the dredging of the St. Lawrence River, enabling heavy-tonnage ships to reach Montréal and eliminating the advantage of unloading in Québec City. The capital's importance began to

History

decline in favour of Montréal, which had an excellent railway system that further helped establish it as the centre of industrial and economic power in Québec and Canada.

The 19th century also saw the advent of the city's first modern municipal government structures. Around 1830, Québec City was divided into 10 districts, each administered by two city councillors who assisted the mayor in his functions. The municipality governed such matters as firefighting, policing, roadwork, markets, gas and water.

The greater Québec City region grew in importance around the middle of the 19th century, as new municipalities were created: Beauport, Saint-Augustin-de-Desmaures, Saint-Félix-de-Cap-Rouge, Sillery, Saint-Ambroise-de-la-Jeune-Lorette, L'Ancienne-Lorette, Sainte-Foy and Charlesbourg. The parish of Saint-Roch, then considered the city's outskirts, included the neighbourhoods of Limoilou and Saint-Sauveur, among others.

Québec City was already delighting wealthy American visitors when the arrival of steamships considerably reduced travel time across the Atlantic, bringing Europeans in droves to visit the "Gibraltar of America."

◀ Loyalists fleeing the American War of Independence arrive in 1783. ©Library and Archives Canada/C-000168

400 YEARS OF FRENCH CULTURE AND PRESENCE IN THE AMERICAS

Founded on July 3, 1608, Québec City, the cradle of French civilization in the Americas, whose historic district of Vieux-Québec has been a UNESCO World Heritage Site since 1985, went all out to celebrate its 400th anniversary in 2008. The capital took advantage of the festivities to undergo a major facelift before receiving its guests. The Promenade Samuel-De Champlain is one of the fruits of that initiative.

There were numerous festivities throughout the year; the Plains of Abraham hosted concerts by Céline Dion and former Beatle Paul McCartney. But the most popular event of the summer was Robert Lepage's *The Image Mill (Moulin à images)*, the world's largest multimedia show. Other popular free shows included *Paris-Québec à travers la chanson* and *Pleins feux sur l'OSQ*.

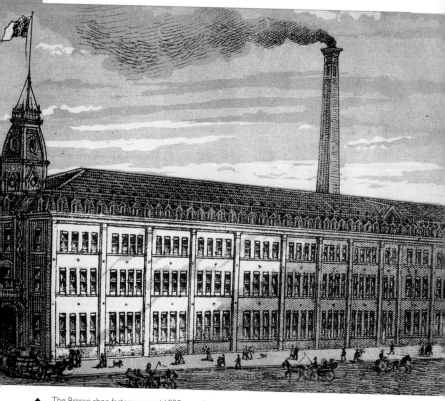

▲ The Bresse shoe factory around 1880, now known as La Fabrique.
©[ca 1887]. AVQ, Fonds de Thérèse Caron, N010083

The 20th Century

Although Québec City lost its economic importance at the beginning of the 20th century and was now limited to light industry such as footwear, concentrated in the Saint-Roch district, it continued to play a significant role in politics and administration as the capital of the province of Québec. The civil service grew in importance and generated economic growth in the construction, retail and service industries.

The turn of the 20th century saw the creation of a robust railway network linking the capital to Montréal; later, the increase in automobile traffic following the First World War spurred the construction of what was an extensive road network for the period. Despite two deadly collapses during its construction, the Québec Bridge was opened in 1917 between Québec City, on the north bank of the St. Lawrence, and Lévis on the south. It was then the longest cantilever bridge in the world. With buses, streetcars, trains and cars allowing people to get around more quickly, new suburbs appeared in the mid-20th century.

This state of affairs continued until the *Révolution Tranquille* (Quiet Revolution) in the 1960s. This social and political "revolution" marked the end of a long period spent under the yoke of religion and tradition, and set the province astir. Morals and

History

▲ Student demonstration during the *Révolution Tranquille*. ©[1968]. AVQ/ Service de police/ N009740

institutions were modernized; political habits evolved. The province of Québec saw the size of its government increase remarkably and Québec City, at the centre of this wave of change, was transformed as well.

At the same time, the nationalist movement made its appearance in Québec as the province's francophones expressed their desire to end the anglophone minority's control over the development of Québec society. During this period, Québec City's anglophone population began to decline, soon representing only 1 or 2% of the region's total population.

Government cutbacks and the decentralization of power to Montréal and the regions have affected employment stability in the area. Although unemployment in Québec City is fairly low, the city now relies mostly on its great industrial and technological potential. In fact, Québec City has a market of more than 500,000 consumers.

Tourism is another major source of revenue, with various tourist attractions such as Vieux-Québec, Mont Sainte-Anne and Montmorency Falls. Hotels have mushroomed along the main highways into town. But one of the most promising areas of economic development remains the advanced technology sector, including biotechnology, computers, optics and telecommunications.

History

QUÉBEC'S EMBLEMS

The *Act respecting the flag and emblems of Québec*, adopted on October 28, 1999 by the National Assembly of Québec, named the blue flag iris (*Iris versicolor* Linnaeus) as the province's official flower. This indigenous flower blossoms in late spring and early summer over much of Québec, from the St. Lawrence River valley to the shores of James Bay.

To commemorate the central role of the forest in the lives of Quebecers, in December 1993 the government named the yellow birch (*Betula alleghaniensis Britton*) the official tree of Québec. Used since the early days of New France, the yellow birch is a mainstay of forests throughout Québec, and is prized for its versatility and commercial value.

Chosen in November 1987 as the official bird of Québec, the snowy owl (*Nyctea scandiaca*) is one of the most beautiful birds in North America. This arctic owl evokes the whiteness of Québec winters and the deep roots of the people of Québec throughout their vast territory despite the harsh climate. The snowy owl nests throughout the tundra, notably on the shores of Ungava Bay.

▲ The snowy owl, official bird of Québec.
©Dreamstime.com/Andrezej Fryda

▲ Iris versicolor. ©Shutterstock/Jennifer Cruz

▲ Yellow birch. ©Sang Hyun (Kevin) Kim

▲ Present-day Québec City. ©*Philippe Renault*

QUÉBEC CITY TODAY

Green Québec City

The Jardin des Gouverneurs, near the Château Frontenac, was once the private garden of the Governor of New France; the Jardins de l'Hôtel-de-Ville, surrounding the city hall, host numerous shows in summertime; the Jardin Jeanne-d'Arc, in the shadow of the Plains of Abraham, is dominated by a statue of the Maid of Orleans astride a powerful charger, amid beautiful flowerbeds; the charming gardens of the Maison Henry-Stuart, headquarters of the Conseil des Monuments et Sites du Québec, are one of a kind; and the Jardin de Saint-Roch, in the neighbourhood of the same name, is gracefully landscaped for the pleasure of passers-by. Finally, at the Bois-de-Coulonge, you can enjoy a stroll through the beautiful flower gardens and the arboretum.

Québec City Today

▲ Panoramic view of Québec City in winter. *©Sylvain Cousineau*

Panoramic Québec City

The Observatoire de la Capitale, atop the Édifice Marie-Guyart in the provincial government's Complexe G, provides an amazing view of the city; the panoramic elevator of the Hôtel Loews Le Concorde runs up to L'Astral rotating restaurant, for another phenomenal view; to say nothing of the breathtaking panoramas from the public promenades and restaurants along the river. A postcard-perfect view is in store for passengers on the ferry between Lévis and the capital. Finally, since 1879 the Funiculaire du Vieux-Québec has offered a splendidly unique view of the river and Basse-Ville.

Artistic Québec City

The 35 historical characters in the beautiful Fresque du Petit-Champlain mural tell the history of Québec City and the Petit-Champlain neighbourhood in particular, while the colourful Fresque des Québécois mural covers 420m² with realistic and instructive figures recounting the saga of the people of Québec.

Festive Québec City

The Carnaval de Québec delights all of Québec City every year with its friendly mascot Bonhomme Carnaval, its ice palace, its nighttime parade, its ice canoe ride across the river and its snow sculpture contest; while the Fêtes de la Nouvelle-France carry visitors back to the foundation of the colony, with period costumes, a recreated market on Place Royale, and a grand costume parade. The Festival d'Été de Québec gets the whole city dancing to the music of artists from around the world, in both indoor and outdoor concerts; and the Grands Feux Loto-Québec firework festival lights up the night with dazzling bursts of colour above the Parc de la Chute-Montmorency, to the delight of the crowd in the park and the yachters and cruise ships on the St. Lawrence below the waterfall.

Québec City Today

▶ A spectacular example of *trompe l'œil*, the Fresque des Québécois. *©David Brisebois*

▶ Bonhomme Carnaval, the Carnaval de Québec mascot. *©Carnaval de Québec*

EXPLORING

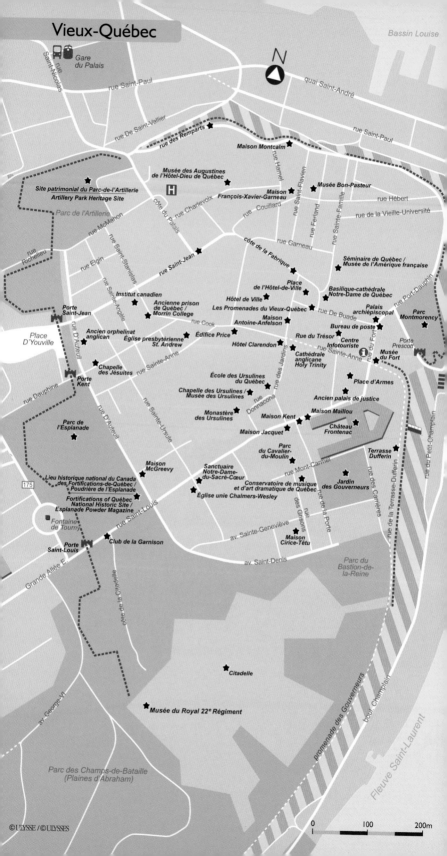

Vieux-Québec

The foremost of Québec City's tourist attractions is a simple stroll through the cobblestone streets of Vieux-Québec. Rain, snow or shine, the old city never fails to delight tourists and residents alike, with its grand attractions, its welcoming cafés and the delicious aromas of its fine restaurants. Its beauty is not only in the age-old stones of the walled city, but also in the warmth and courtesy of its inhabitants.

Vieux-Québec is divided into two parts by Cap Diamant. The part that spreads out between the river and the cliff is featured in the chapters "Petit-Champlain and Place-Royale" and "Vieux-Port". The section covering the plateau atop Cap Diamant is informally called Vieux-Québec. As the administrative and institutional centre of the city, it is adorned with convents, chapels and public buildings some of which date back to the 17th century. The walls of Haute-Ville, dominated by the Citadelle, surround this section of Vieux-Québec and give it the look of a fortress. These same walls long held the development of the town in check, resulting in a densely built-up bourgeois and aristocratic milieu. Over time, the picturesque urban planning of the 19th century contributed to the present-day image of Québec City through the construction of such magnificent buildings as the Château Frontenac and the creation of such public spaces as Terrasse Dufferin, in the *belle époque* spirit.

The **Porte Saint-Louis** gateway is the result of Québec City merchants' pressure on the government between 1870 and 1875 to tear down the wall surrounding the city. The Governor General of Canada at the time, Lord Dufferin, was opposed to the idea and instead put forward a plan drafted by Irishman William H. Lynn to showcase the walls while improving traffic circulation. The design he submitted exhibits a Victorian romanticism in its use of grand gateways that bring to mind images of medieval castles and horsemen. The pepper-box tower of Porte Saint-Louis, built in 1878, makes for a striking first impression upon arriving in downtown Québec City.

Past Porte Saint-Louis, facing Parc de l'Esplanade, are the busts of British Prime Minister Winston Churchill and U.S. President Franklin D. Roosevelt. The two statues commemorate the Québec Conferences that were held by the Allies in 1943 and 1944.

On the right, on the opposite side of the street, is the **Garrison Club**, reserved for army officers, as well as the road leading to the Citadelle.

Québec City's **Citadelle** (citadel) represents three centuries of North American military history and is still in use. Since 1920, it has housed the Royal 22e Régiment of the Canadian Army (nicknamed the *Vandoos* in English), a regiment distinguished for its bravery during World War II. Within the enclosure are some 25 buildings, including the officers' mess, the hospital, the prison and the official Québec City residence of the Governor General of Canada, as well as the first observatory in Canada. The Citadelle's history began in 1693, when engineer Dubois Berthelot de Beaucours had the Cap Diamant redoubt built at the highest point of Québec City's defensive system, some 100m above the river. Today, this solid construction is part of the King's bastion.

Throughout the 18th century, French and then British engineers developed projects for a citadel that remained uncompleted.

▼ The Porte Saint-Louis gateway. ©Philippe Renault/Hemis

▲   A Citadelle soldier in dress uniform. ©Dreamstime.com/Gary Blakeley

Chaussegros de Léry's powder house of 1750, which now houses the Museum of the Royal 22ᵉ Régiment, and the temporary excavation works to the west (1783) are the only works of any scope accomplished during this period. The citadel as it exists today was built between 1820 and 1832 by Colonel Elias Walker Durnford according to principles expounded by Vauban in the 17th century. Though this defensive structure led to Québec being dubbed the "Gibraltar of America," it never actually bore the brunt of a single cannonball, though it certainly had a dissuasive effect.

The **Musée du Royal 22ᵉ Régiment** is a museum that offers an interesting collection of weapons, uniforms, insignia and military documents spanning almost 400 years. In summer, guided tours of the whole installation are offered daily, where you'll witness the changing of the guard, the retreat, and the firing of the cannon.

The **Fortifications of Québec National Historic Site** displays models and maps outlining the development of Québec City's defence system in the interpretive centre; you can also visit the **Esplanade Powder Magazine** (Poudrière de l'Esplanade). Interpretive plaques have been placed along the top of the wall, providing another means of discovering the city's history. The walkway on top of the wall can be reached by using the stairs next to the city gates.

Vieux-Québec

IN THE SPOTLIGHT

Inspired by other great cities of the world, Québec City set up its own lighting plan during the 1990s. Now, when night falls, a carefully planned lighting system illuminates the capital's most beautiful monuments and natural sites, to make the setting even more beautiful for residents and visitors alike. Some 20 monuments and sites now shine forth under the starry sky, out of a planned 70. Keep your eyes open and enjoy the breathtaking sights!

▶ The Édifice Price at night.
©istockphoto.com/Gary Martin

Québec City's first wall was made of earth and wooden posts. It was erected on the west side of the city in 1693, according to the plans of engineer Dubois Berthelot de Beaucours, to protect Québec City from the Iroquois. Work on much stronger stone fortifications, designed by engineer Chaussegros de Léry, began in 1745 when England and France entered a new period of conflict. However, the wall remained unfinished when the city was seized by the British in 1759. The British saw to the completion of the project at the end of the 18th century. Some work on the Citadelle began in 1693; however, the structure as we now know it was essentially built between 1820 and 1832. Nevertheless, the Citadelle is largely designed according to the principles advanced by Vauban in the 17th century—principles that suit the location admirably.

Until the end of the 19th century, Québec City had a small but influential community of Scottish Presbyterians, most of whom were involved in shipping and the lumber trade. The **Chalmers-Wesley United Church**, an attractive Gothic Revival structure now shared with the francophone parish of Saint-Pierre, testifies to the past vitality of the Scottish Presbyterian community.

Vieux-Québec

◀ The Fortifications of Québec National Historic Site. ©Parks Canada, B. Ostiguy

The church was built in 1852 and designed by John Wells, an architect known for a number of famous buildings, including the Bank of Montreal headquarters (1847). The elegant Gothic Revival spire of the church contributes to the picturesque appearance of the city. The church's organ dates back to 1890 and was restored in 1985. During World War II, a radio station transmitted a half-hour organ recital live every Sunday night. Today, concerts such as choir recitals are presented at the church year round.

The **Sanctuaire Notre-Dame-du-Sacré-Coeur** faces Chalmers-Wesley United Church. The sanctuary was originally built for the Sacré Cœur missionaries. This place of worship, erected in 1910 and designed by François-Xavier Berlinguet, is now open to everyone. The sanctuary has a Gothic Revival facade. Its two rather narrow steeples seem dwarfed by the size of the building. The interior of the structure, with its stained glass windows and ex-votos, is more attractive.

In addition to the city's major historical landmarks, Québec's appeal lies in its smaller, less imposing buildings, each of which has its own individual history. It is a delight to simply wander the narrow streets of the old city, taking in the subtleties of an architecture so atypical of North America. At 25 Avenue Sainte-Geneviève, the **Maison Cirice-Têtu** was built in 1852. It was designed by Charles Baillairgé, a member of a celebrated family of architects who, beginning in the 18th century, left an important mark on the architecture of Québec City and its surroundings. The Greek Revival facade of the house, a masterpiece of the genre, is tastefully decorated with palmettes and discreet laurel wreaths. The main floor has huge bay windows that open onto a single expansive living room in the London style. From the time of its construction, the house incorporated all the modern amenities: central heating, hot running water and multiple bathrooms. The De Koninck family hosted Antoine de Saint-Exupéry, author of *The Little Prince*, in this house in the early 1940s.

A short detour onto Rue des Grisons brings you to the end of Rue Mont-Carmel and one of the remnants of Québec City's earliest fortifications, the **Cavalier du Moulin** (1693), in an out-of-the-way spot behind a row of houses.

◀ The Sanctuaire Notre-Dame-du-Sacré-Cœur.
©Philippe Renault/Hemis

▶ Terrasse Dufferin, the city's most beautiful boardwalk. ©istockphoto.com/Tony Tremblay

SMALL PANES OF GLASS

Why do the windows of the old houses in Québec City and the rest of the province have several small panes of glass instead of one large one? You might think it is because of the cold and the snow. But the answer is even more down-to-earth. During colonial times, glass had to be imported from France. Needless to say, much of it was broken en route.

As a result, the merchants decided to import smaller pieces of glass so there would be less risk of breakage during the transatlantic crossing. Furthermore, they were sometimes transported in large barrels of molasses for added protection!

A *cavalier* is a redoubt set within the city walls from which the walls could be destroyed in the event of a successful enemy invasion. The fortification is named for the windmill, or *moulin*, that used to sit on top of it. Today, the **Parc du Cavalier-du-Moulin** provides a pleasant spot for relaxing amid the benches, cannons, and promenade. Facing the park at 3 Rue des Grisons is the Conservatoire de Musique et d'Art Dramatique de Québec.

The charming square known as **Jardin des Gouverneurs** was originally the private garden of the governor of New France. The square was laid out in 1647 for Charles Huaut de Montmagny to the west of Château Saint-Louis, the residence of the governor, which no longer exists. A monument to opposing military leaders Wolfe and Montcalm, both of whom died on the battlefields of the Plains of Abraham, was erected during the restoration of the garden in 1827.

A walk on the wooden planks of the **Terrasse Dufferin**, overlooking the St. Lawrence River, provides a different sensation than the pavement we are used

◀ A monument to Wolfe and Montcalm in the Jardin des Gouverneurs. ©Philippe Renault/Hemis

to. It was built in 1879 at the request of the governor general of the time, Lord Dufferin. The boardwalk's open-air pavilions and ornate streetlamps were designed by Charles Baillairgé and were inspired by the style of French urban architecture that was common under Napoleon III. Terrasse Dufferin is one of Québec City's most popular sights and is the preferred meeting place for young people. The view of the river, the south shore and Île d'Orléans is magnificent. During the winter months, a huge ice slide is set up at the western end of the boardwalk.

Terrasse Dufferin is located where the Château Saint-Louis, the elaborate residence of the governor of New France, once stood. Built at the very edge of the escarpment, this three-storey building had a long, private stone terrace on the river side, while the main entrance, consisting of a fortified facade, opened onto Place d'Armes and featured pavilions with imperial-type roofs. The château was built in the 17th century and was

enlarged in 1719. Its rooms, linked one to the other, were the scene of elegant receptions given for the French nobility. Plans for the future of the entire continent were drawn up in this building. Château Saint-Louis was badly damaged in the British invasion of the city at the time of the Conquest and was later remodelled according to British tastes, before being destroyed by a fire in 1834.

There are two monuments at the far end of Terrasse Dufferin. One is dedicated to the memory of Samuel de Champlain, the founder of Québec City and father of New France. It was designed by Parisian sculptor Paul Chevré and erected in 1898. The second monument informs visitors that Vieux-Québec was recognized as a World Heritage Site by UNESCO in 1985. Québec City was the first city in North America to be added to this list. A staircase just to the left of the Champlain monument leads to the Place-Royale sector. At the other end of the Terrasse, you'll find another staircase leading to the Promenade des Gouverneurs.

The first half of the 19th century saw the emergence of Québec City's tourism industry when the romantic European nature of the city began to attract growing numbers of American visitors. In 1890, the Canadian Pacific Railway company, under Cornelius Van Horne, decided to create a chain of distinguished hotels across Canada. The first of these hotels was the **Château Frontenac**, named in honour of one of the best-known governors of New France, Louis de Buade, comte de Frontenac (1622-1698).

The magnificent Château Frontenac, symbol of the province's capital city, is the most famous sight in Québec. Ironically, the hotel was designed by an American architect, Bruce Price (1845-1903) who was known for his New York skyscrapers. The look of the hotel, which combines certain elements of Scottish manors and the châteaux of the Loire Valley in France, has come to be considered a national archetype style called "Château Style." Bruce Price, who also designed Montréal's Windsor train station (1889), was inspired by the picturesque

▼   Château Frontenac in all its splendour. ©istockphoto.com/Andre Nantel

location that was chosen for the hotel and by the mix of French and English cultures in Canada.

The Château Frontenac was built in phases. Price's initial wing overlooked Terrasse Dufferin and was completed in 1893. Three sections were later added, the most important of these being the central tower (1923). To fully appreciate the château, one must go inside to explore the main hall, decorated in a style popular in 18th-century Parisian *hôtels particuliers*, and visit the Bar Maritime in the large

main tower overlooking the river. The Château Frontenac has been the site of a number of important events in history. In 1944, the Québec Conference was held here. At this historic meeting, U.S. President Franklin D. Roosevelt, British Prime Minister Winston Churchill and Canadian Prime Minister Mackenzie King met to discuss the future of post-war Europe. On the way out of the courtyard is a stone with the inscription of the Order of Malta, dated 1647, the only remaining piece of Château Saint-Louis. Tours of Château Frontenac are given by guides portraying historical figures, dressed in period costumes.

Until the construction of the Citadelle, **Place d'Armes** was a military parade ground. It became a public square in 1865. In 1916, the *Monument de la Foi* (Monument of Faith) was erected in Place d'Armes to mark the tricentennial of the arrival of the Récollet religious order in Québec. Abbot Adolphe Garneau's statue rests on a base designed by David Ouellet.

The **Centre Infotouriste** is located in the former Union Hotel, a white building with a copper roof on Rue Sainte-Anne. A group of wealthy Quebecers saw the need for a luxury hotel in Québec City, and the project was completed in 1803.

Near the Centre Infotouriste is one of Québec City's traditional tourist attractions, the **Musée du Fort**. The museum uses an elaborate model of the city and a sound and light show to recreate the six sieges of Québec City, starting with the capture of the town by the Kirke brothers in 1629, continuing through the Battle of the Plains of Abraham in 1759, and ending with the American invasion of 1775.

The former **Palais de Justice (Courthouse)** is the city's original courthouse, built in 1883 by Eugène-Étienne Taché, also the architect of the parliament buildings. The courthouse resembles the

Vieux-Québec

parliament in a number of ways. Its French Renaissance Revival design preceded the Château style as the "official" style of the city's major building projects. The interior of the building was renovated between 1922 and 1930; it has several large rooms with attractive woodwork. The Ancien

◀ Place d'Armes and its Monument de la Foi.
©Philippe Renault/Hemis

◀ The Musée du Fort's elaborate model of the city circa 1750. ©Étienne Boucher

▼ Built in 1675, Maison Jacquet now houses a renowned restaurant. ©Philippe Renault/Hemis

Palais de Justice building, now known as Édifice Gérard-D.-Lévesque, is home to Québec's Ministère des finances.

At 17 Rue Saint-Louis, **Maison Maillou** houses Québec City's chamber of commerce. This attractive French Regime house was built in 1736 by architect Jean Maillou. It was saved from demolition when the stock market crash of 1929 led to the abandonment of plans to expand the Château Frontenac.

The history of **Maison Kent** is somewhat cloudy. Located at 25 Rue Saint-Louis, it was once a residence of Queen Victoria's father, the Duke of Kent. There is some disagreement as to whether the house was built in the 17th or 18th century. It is clear, however, from its English sash windows and low-pitched roof, that the house underwent major renovations during the 19th century. The agreement that handed Québec City over to the British in 1759 was signed in this house. Ironically, it is now occupied by the Consulate General of France.

Maison Jacquet, a small, red-roofed building covered in white roughcast, is the oldest house in Haute-Ville; it is the only house in Vieux-Québec that still looks just as it did in the 17th century. The house is distinguished from those built during the following century by its high, steep roof covering a living area with a very low ceiling. The house is named for François Jacquet, who once owned the land on which it stands. It was built by architect François de la Joüe in 1675, for his own use. In 1815, the house was acquired by Philippe Aubert de Gaspé, author of the famous novel *Les Anciens Canadiens* (The Canadians of Old).

At the corner of tiny Rue du Parloir and Rue Donnacona, you will find the **Monastère des Ursulines**. In 1535, St. Angela Merici founded the first Ursuline community in Brescia, Italy. After the community had established itself in France,

Vieux-Québec

it became a cloistered order dedicated to teaching (1620). With the help of a benefactor, Madame de la Peltrie, the Ursulines arrived in Québec City in 1639 and, in 1641, founded a monastery and convent where generations of young girls have received a good education. The **École des Ursulines du Québec** is the longest-running girls' school in North America. Only the museum and chapel, a small part of the huge Ursulines complex where several dozen nuns still live, are open to the public.

The **Sainte-Ursuline chapel** was rebuilt in 1901 on the site of the original 1722 chapel. Part of the magnificent interior decoration of the first chapel, created by Pierre-Nöel Levasseur between 1726 and 1736, survived and is present in the newer structure. The work includes a pulpit surmounted by a trumpeting angel and a beautiful altarpiece in the Louis XIV style. The tabernacle of the high altar is embellished with fine gilding applied by the Ursulines. The Sacred Heart tabernacle, a masterpiece of the genre, is attributed to Jacques Leblond dit Latour, and dates from around 1770. Some of the paintings decorating the church come from the collection of Father Jean-Louis Desjardins, a former chaplain of the Ursulines. In 1820, Desjardins bought several dozen paintings from an art dealer in Paris. The paintings had previously hung in Paris churches but were removed during the French Revolution. Works from this collection can still be seen in churches all over Québec. At the entrance hangs *Jésus chez Simon le Pharisien* (Jesus with Simon the Pharisee) by Philippe de Champaigne, and to the right of the nave hangs *La Parabole des Dix Vierges* (The Parable of the Ten Virgins), by Pierre de Cortone.

▲ Inside the Sainte-Ursuline chapel.
©Philippe Renault/Hemis

▲ The entrance to the Sainte-Ursuline chapel.
©Philippe Renault/Hemis

The chapel was the burial site of the Marquis de Montcalm until 2001, when his remains were transferred to the military cemetery at the Hôpital Général. Commander of the French troops during the decisive Battle of the Plains of Abraham, he was fatally wounded during the conflict, as was his rival General Wolfe. The tomb of Blessed Mère Marie de l'Incarnation, the founder of the Ursulines monastery in Québec City, is still there. An opening provides a view of the nuns' chancel, rebuilt in 1902 by David Ouellet, who outfitted it with a cupola-shaped skylight. An interesting painting by an unknown artist, *La France Apportant la Foi aux Indiens de la Nouvelle-France* (France Bringing the Faith to the Indians of New France), also hangs in this section of the chapel.

◄ The superb Monastère des Ursulines convent. ©Philippe Renault/Hemis

Vieux-Québec

The entrance to the **Musée des Ursulines** is located across from the chapel. The museum outlines nearly four centuries of Ursuline history. On view are various works of art, Louis XIII furniture, impressive embroideries made of gold thread, and 18th-century altar cloths and church robes.

After the British Conquest of Québec, a small group of British administrators and military officers established themselves in Québec City. These men wanted to mark their presence through the construction of prestigious buildings with typically British designs. However, their small numbers resulted in the slow progress of this project until the beginning of the 19th century, when work began on the **Holy Trinity Anglican Cathedral** by two military engineers inspired by St. Martin in the Fields Church in London. The Palladian-style church was completed in 1804. This significant example of non-French architecture changed the look of the city. The church was the first Anglican cathedral built outside Britain and, in its elegant simplicity, is a good example of British colonial architecture. The roof was made steeper in 1815 so that it would not be weighed down by snow.

The cathedral's interior, soberer than that of most Catholic churches, is adorned with various generous gifts from King George III, including several pieces of

▶   The pretty Holy Trinity Anglican Cathedral.
    ©David Paul Ohmer

HOMAGE TO THE BAILLAIRGÉ FAMILY

In 2004, a monument was inaugurated on Chaussée des Écossais, in front of Morrin College, commemorating four generations of the Baillairgé family of artists and architects, who did so much to shape the face of Québec City.

From 1750 to 1900, the Baillairgés enriched the religious heritage of Québec, especially in the capital region, designing, planning, building, and decorating more than 150 religious buildings including cathedrals, churches, and convent and hospital chapels.

The family's most eminent member, architect Thomas Baillairgé (1791-1859), planned more than a hundred churches, institutional buildings, and residences. His influence also transformed architecture in Québec from a craft to a profession. In collaboration with the religious authorities of the time, in particular Abbé Jérôme Demers, he developed an original architectural style for the province.

silverware and pews made of English oak from the forests of Windsor. The bishop's chair is said to have been carved from an elm tree under which Samuel de Champlain liked to sit. There are stained-glass windows and commemorative plaques added over the years, and a Casavant organ dating from 1909 that was restored in 1959. The church's set of eight bells is one of the oldest in Canada.

The **Hôtel Clarendon** began receiving guests in 1870 in the former Desbarats print shop (1858). It is the oldest hotel still operating in Québec City. The restaurant Le Charles Baillairgé on the main floor is also the oldest restaurant in Canada. The Victorian charm of the sombre woodwork evokes the *belle époque*. The Hôtel Clarendon was expanded in 1929 by the addition of a brick tower featuring an Art Deco entrance hall designed by Raoul Chênevert.

When Montréal architects Ross and MacDonald designed the **Édifice Price** in 1929, they managed to create a traditional North American skyscraper that does not look out of place among the historic buildings of the Haute-Ville. The tall yet discreet building features a copper roof typical of Château-style architecture. The main hall of the building, a fine example of Art Deco design, is covered in polished travertine and bronze bas-reliefs depicting the various activities of the Price paper company.

Further along Rue Sainte-Anne, near the Édifice Price, a granite and bronze sculpture by Jules Lasalle entitled *L'Envol* pays homage to the priests and nuns who taught Québec children for centuries.

The next stop is quaint **Maison Antoine-Anfelson** at 17 Rue des Jardins, built in 1780. A talented silversmith by the name of Laurent Amiot had a workshop here

▲ The attractive Hôtel de Ville (1896).
©Gilbert Bochenek

in the 19th century. The rooms on the second floor of this building feature wonderful Louis XV woodwork.

Place de l'Hôtel-de-Ville, a small square, was the location of the Notre-Dame market in the 18th century. A monument in honour of Cardinal Taschereau, created by André Vermare, was erected here in 1923.

The American Romanesque Revival influence seen in the **Hôtel de Ville** stands out in a city where French and British traditions have always dominated the construction of public buildings. The building was designed by George-Émile Tanguay in 1895 following disagreements among the mayor and the city councillors

▲ The Art Deco entrance hall at Hôtel Clarendon. ©Philippe Renault/Hemis

as to a building plan. Sadly, a Jesuit college dating from 1666 was demolished to make room for the city hall.

Under the pleasant **Jardins de l'Hôtel-de-Ville**, the gardens where popular events are held in the summer, is an underground parking lot, a much needed addition in this city of narrow streets.

The **Basilique-Cathédrale Notre-Dame-de-Québec** as it stands today is the result of numerous phases of construction and a number of tragedies that left the church in ruins on two occasions. The first church on this site was built in 1632 under the orders of Samuel de Champlain, who was buried nearby four years later. This wooden church was replaced in 1647 by the Église Notre-Dame-de-la-Paix, a stone church in the shape of a Roman cross that would later serve as the model for many rural parish churches. In 1674, New France was assigned its first bishop in residence. Monseigneur François-Xavier de Montmorency-Laval (1623-1708) decided that this small church, after renovations befitting its status as the heart of such an enormous ministry, would become the seat of the Catholic Church in Québec. Only the base of the west tower survives from this period. In 1742, the bishop had the church remodelled, featuring an extended nave illuminated from above. The cathedral resembles many urban churches built in France during the same period.

During the siege of Québec in 1759, the cathedral was bombarded, suffering severe damage. It was not restored until the status of Catholics in Québec was settled by the British crown. The oldest Catholic parish north of Mexico was finally allowed to begin the reconstruction of its church in 1770, using the 1742 plans. The work was directed by Jean Baillairgé (1726-1805). In 1786, the decoration of the church's interior was entrusted to Jean Baillairgé's son François (1759-1830), who had recently returned from three years of studying architecture in Paris at the Académie Royale. He designed the chancel's beautiful gilt canopy with winged caryatids four years later. The high altar, the first in Québec to be designed to look like the facade

Vieux-Québec

◄   The Basilique-Cathédrale Notre-Dame-de-Québec and Place de l'Hôtel-de-Ville.
©Philippe Renault/Hemis

of a basilica, was installed in 1797. The addition of baroque pews and a plaster vault created an interesting contrast. Thus completed, the spectacular interior emphasized the use of gilding, wood and white plasterwork according to traditional Québécois decor.

In 1843, Thomas Baillairgé (1791-1859), the son of François, created the present neoclassical facade. Charles Baillairgé (1826-1906), Thomas Baillairgé's cousin, designed the wrought-iron gate around the front square in 1858. Between 1920 and 1922, the church was carefully restored, but just a few weeks after the work was completed a fire devastated the building. Raoul Chênevert and Maxime Roisin, who had already come to Québec from Paris to take on the reconstruc-

tion of the Basilica in Sainte-Anne-de-Beaupré, were put in charge of another restoration of the cathedral. In 1959, a mausoleum was added in the basement of the church. It holds the remains of the Bishops of Québec and various governors (Frontenac, Vaudreuil, de Callière and Jonquière).

During the 17th century, the **Séminaire de Québec** religious complex was an oasis of European civilization in a rugged and hostile territory. To get an idea of how it must have appeared to students of the day, go through the old gate (decorated with the seminary's coat of arms) and into the courtyard before proceeding through the opposite entryway to the reception desk.

▼   The historic Séminaire de Québec. ©Philippe Renault/Hemis

The seminary was founded in 1663 by Monseigneur François de Montmorency-Laval, on orders from the Séminaire des Missions Étrangères de Paris (seminary of foreign missions), with which it remained affiliated until 1763. As headquarters of the clergy throughout the colony, it was at the seminary that future priests studied, that parochial funds were administered, and that ministerial appointments were made. Louis XIV's minister Colbert further required the seminary to establish a smaller school devoted to the conversion and education of native people. Following the British Conquest and the subsequent banishment of the Jesuits, the seminary became a college devoted to classical education. It also served as a residence for the bishop of Québec after his palace was destroyed during the invasion. In 1852, the seminary founded Université Laval, the first French-language university in North America. The Séminaire's vast ensemble of buildings now includes the priests' residence, a private school for boys and girls, the Université Laval school of architecture, and the Musée de l'Amérique Française.

Today's seminary is the result of rebuilding efforts following numerous fires and bombardments. Across from the old gate the wing devoted to the offices of the Procurator can be seen, complete with sundial. During the 1690 attack of Admiral Phipps, it was in the vaulted cellars of this wing that the citizens of Québec City took refuge. The building also hosts the personal chapel of Mgr. Briand (1785), decorated with sculpted olive branches.

▲ L'Œuvre du Séminaire de Québec, the permanent exhibit at the Musée de l'Amérique Française. ©Idra Labrie

The **Musée de l'Amérique Française** is dedicated to the history of North America's French-speaking peoples revealed through the collections of the priests of the Séminaire de Québec displayed in its permanent exhibit: *L'Œuvre du Séminaire de Québec*, on the social and economic contributions of priests in Québec society. The museum also hosts two temporary exhibits. Occupying former Université Laval residences, its three floors display priceless collections of gold sculpture, paintings, Oriental art, coins and scientific instruments.

Today part of the museum, the outer chapel, built in 1890, has been renamed the "Chapelle du Musée." It replaced a chapel that burned in 1888, itself a replacement for a chapel built in 1752. To avoid another disaster, the interior, similar to that of the Église de la Trinité in Paris, was clad in tin and zinc and painted in *trompe l'oeil*. The chapel contains the largest collection of relics in North America, including those of Saint Augustine, Saint Anselm, the martyrs of Tonkin, Saint Charles Borromée and Saint Ignatius Loyola. Some of the relics are large and authentic while others are small and rather dubious. On the left is a funeral chapel housing a tomb containing the remains of Monseigneur de Laval, the first bishop in North America. Although Mgr. Laval's remains were moved to the cathedral following the deconsecration of the chapel in 1992, his tomb with its sculpted effigy remains.

The old Holt Renfrew store, which opened in 1837, faces the cathedral. The store originally sold furs, which it supplied by appointment to Her Majesty the Queen, and for many years held the exclusive rights for the Canadian distribution of Dior and Yves Saint-Laurent creations. Holt's is now closed, having given way to the boutiques of the **Promenades du Vieux-Québec**, which present an elaborate show depicting the history of Québec City, *Québec Expérience*. This lively three-dimensional multimedia presentation takes viewers back in time to relive the great moments in the city's history through its important historical figures. A wonderful way to learn about Québec City's past, these half-hour shows are a big hit with kids. A little further on is the

▲ The Musée de l'Amérique Française chapel.
©Pierre Soulard

entrance to **Rue du Trésor**, which also leads to Place d'Armes and Rue Sainte-Anne. Artists come here to sell paintings, drawings and silkscreens, many of which depict views of Québec City.

The old **Bureau de Poste** (Post Office) of Québec City, at 3 Passage du Chien-d'Or, was built between 1871 and 1873 on the former site of the Hôtel du Chien d'Or, a sturdy dwelling built around 1735 for a wealthy Bordeaux merchant, who ordered a bas-relief depicting a dog gnawing a bone installed above the doorway. The following inscription appeared underneath the bas-relief, which was relocated to the pediment of the present post office in 1872: *"Je suis un chien qui ronge l'os, en le rongeant je prends mon repos. Un temps viendra qui n'est pas venu où je mordrai qui m'aura mordu."* (I am a dog gnawing a bone, and as I gnaw, I rest at home. Though it's not yet here there'll come a time when those who bit me will be paid in kind.) It is said that the message was meant for Intendant Bigot, a man known for being a swindler, who was so outraged he had the Bordeaux merchant killed.

The dome of the post office and the facade overlooking the river were added at the beginning of the 20th century. The building was renamed Édifice Louis-S.-Saint-Laurent, in honour of the former prime minister of Canada. Besides the usual post and philatelic services, a **Parks Canada Information Office** was added to promote Canada's natural and historical heritage. The entrance to the information office offers a lovely view of the river and the Parc Montmorency.

Near the post office stands a **Monument to Monseigneur François de Montmorency Laval** (1623-1708), the first bishop of Québec, whose diocese covered two thirds of North America. Designed by Louis-Philippe Hébert and erected in 1908, the monument neighbours an attractive staircase that leads to Côte de la Montagne and down to the river.

The monument to Bishop Laval is located directly in front of the **Palais Archiépiscopal** or archbishop's palace, which was rebuilt by Thomas Baillairgé in 1844. The first bishop's palace stood in what is now Parc Montmorency. Built between 1692

Vieux-Québec

and 1700, the original palace was, by all accounts, one of the most gorgeous of its kind in New France. Drawings show an impressive building, complete with a recessed chapel whose interior was reminiscent of Paris's Val-de-Grâce. Though the chapel was destroyed in 1759, the rest of the building was restored and then occupied by the Legislative Assembly of Lower Canada from 1792 to 1840. It was demolished in 1848 to make room for the new parliamentary buildings, which went up in flames only four years later.

Parc Montmorency was laid out in 1875 after the city walls were lowered along Rue des Remparts and the governor general of Canada, Lord Dufferin, discovered the magnificent view from the promontory. George-Étienne Cartier, prime minister of the Dominion of Canada and one of the Fathers of Confederation, is honoured with a statue here, as are Louis Hébert, Guillaume Couillard and Marie Rollet, some of the original settlers of New France. These three landed in 1617 and were granted the fiefdom of Sault-au-Matelot, on the future site of the seminary, in 1623. These attractive bronzes are the work of Montréal sculptor Alfred Laliberté.

RUE DU TRÉSOR, AN ARTISTS' HAVEN

The name of Rue du Trésor is thought to be connected to the Compagnie des Cent-Associés, which administered New France and held a trade monopoly from 1627 to 1663. Their assets were referred to as the "Trésor," a treasure or treasury. At that time, its headquarters was located on Rue Sainte-Anne, near the current site of the Anglican Holy Trinity Cathedral; the little street that led to it was named Rue du Trésor in 1689.

For the last forty years Rue du Trésor has been an open-air art gallery; with the works of some thirty artists (watercolour painters, engravers, etc.) on display, it has become one of the most popular sights in Québec City. As you explore the narrow, winding streets of Vieux-Québec, be sure to take a detour to see this little treasure of a street.

◀ Rue du Trésor, a veritable outdoor art gallery.
©Hélène Huard

▲ A row of cannons in Parc Montmorency.
©Parks Canada, J. Beardsell

▲ The old Bureau de Poste.
©Dreamstime.com/Karen Brandt

The halls of the old Université Laval can be seen through a gap in the ramparts. Built in 1856 in the gardens of the seminary, they were completed in 1875 with the addition of an impressive mansard roof surmounted by three silver lanterns. When the spotlights shine on them at night, it creates the atmosphere of a royal gala. Today, Université Laval occupies a large campus in Sainte-Foy.

Following **Rue des Remparts**, Basse-Ville (the lower town) comes into view and you'll see a lot of old cannons. The patrician manors on the street along the ramparts provide a picturesque backdrop for the old Latin quarter which extends behind them. The narrow streets and 18th-century houses in this neighbourhood are worth a detour.

Maison Montcalm, at 45 to 51 Rue des Remparts, was originally a single very large residence constructed in 1727; it is now divided into three houses. Home to the Marquis de Montcalm at the time of the Battle of the Plains of Abraham, the building subsequently housed the officers of the British army before being subdivided and returned to private use. In the first half of the 19th century, many houses in Québec were covered in the sort of imitation stone boards that still protect the masonry of the Montcalm house. It was believed that this type of covering lent a more refined look to the houses.

At the corner of Rue Couillard is **Maison François-Xavier-Garneau**. Québec City businessman Louis Garneau recently

Vieux-Québec

bought this neoclassical house (1862) where historian and poet François-Xavier Garneau lived during the last years of his life. Throughout the summer, the past comes alive with tours given by guides dressed in period costume.

Nearby, on Rue Couillard, is the **Musée Bon-Pasteur**. Founded in 1993, it tells the story of the Bon Pasteur (Good Shepherd) community of nuns, who have been serving the poor of Québec City since 1850. The museum is located in the Béthanie house, an eclectic brick structure built around 1887 to shelter unwed mothers and their children. The museum occupies three floors of an 1878 addition and houses furniture as well as sacred objects manufactured or collected by the nuns, as well as a video documentary that recounts an adoption.

The Augustinian nurses founded their first Québec convent in Sillery. Uneasy about the Iroquois, they relocated to Québec City in 1642 and began construction of the present complex, the Hôtel-Dieu, which includes a convent, a hospital and a chapel. Rebuilt several times, today's buildings mostly date from the 20th century. The oldest remaining part is the 1756 convent, built on the vaulted foundations from 1695 and hidden behind the 1800 chapel. This chapel was erected using material from various French buildings destroyed during the Seven Years' War. The stone was taken from the palace of the intendant, while its first ornaments came from the 17th-century Jesuit church. Today, only the iron balustrade of the bell tower bears witness to the original chapel. The present neoclassical facade was designed by Thomas Baillairgé in 1839 after he completed the new interior in 1835.

Vieux-Québec

▸ Rue des Remparts and its old cannons. ©Philippe Renault/Hemis

The **Musée des Augustines du Monastère de l'Hôtel-Dieu** is a museum which traces the history of the Augustinian community in New France through pieces of furniture, paintings and medical instruments. On display is the chest that contained the meagre belongings of the founders (pre-1639), as well as pieces from the Château Saint-Louis, the residence of the first governors under the French Regime, including portraits of Louis XIV and Cardinal Richelieu. Upon request, visitors can see the chapel and the vaulted cellars. The remains of Blessed Marie-Catherine de Saint-Augustin, the founder of the community in New France, are kept in an adjoining chapel, as is a beautiful gilded reliquary in the Louis XIV style, sculpted in 1717 by Pierre-Noël Levasseur.

At the corner of Rue Saint-Jean and Rue de l'Hôtel-Dieu, visitors can get a pleasant view of the **Côte de la Fabrique**, with the Hôtel de Ville on the right and

▼ The magnificent Musée Bon-Pasteur. ©*Patrick Escudero*

Basilique-Cathédrale Notre-Dame in the background on the left. **Rue Saint-Jean**, which runs westward, is a lovely commercial street.

A short detour to the left down Rue Saint-Stanislas provides a view of the old Methodist church, a beautiful Gothic Revival building dating from 1850. Today it houses the **Institut Canadien**, a centre for literature and the arts. Before the Quiet Revolution of the 1960s, this centre was the focus of many a contentious dispute with the clergy over its "audacious" choice of books.

The neighbouring building, number 44, is the former **Prison de Québec** (jail) built in 1808. In 1868 it was renovated to accommodate **Morrin College**, affiliated with Montréal's McGill University. This venerable institution of English-speaking Québec also houses the library of the **Literary and Historical Society of Québec**, a learned society founded in 1824.

The portion of Rue Saint-Stanislas located between Rue Sainte-Anne and the Institut Canadien was renamed "Chaussée des Écossais" (Scots' Road) in 2000.

The building on the corner of Rue Cook and Rue Dauphine, topped by a Palladian steeple, is **St. Andrew's Presbyterian Church**, completed in 1811.

Artillery Park Heritage Site / Site Patrimonial du Parc-de-l'Artillerie includes part of an enormous military installation running alongside the walls of the city. The reception and information centre is located in the old foundry where munitions were manufactured until 1964. On display is a fascinating model of Québec City, which was built between 1795 and 1810 by military engineer Jean-Baptiste Duberger for strategic planning. The model has only recently been returned to Québec City, after having been sent to England in 1813. It is an unparalleled

▲ The famous Côte de la Fabrique. ©Hélène Huard

▲ The Musée des Augustines du Monastère de l'Hôtel-Dieu.
©Conseil du patrimoine religieux du Québec, 2003

source of information on the layout of the city in the years following the British Conquest.

The walk continues with a visit to the **Dauphine Redoubt**, a beautiful white roughcast building near Rue McMahon. In 1712, military engineer Dubois Berthelot de Beaucours drafted plans for the redoubt, which was completed by Chaussegros de Léry in 1747. A redoubt is an independent fortified structure that serves as a retreat in case the troops are obliged to fall back. The redoubt was

Vieux-Québec

never actually used for this purpose, but rather as a military barracks. Behind it are several barracks and an old cartridge factory constructed by the British in the 19th century. The officers' barracks (1820), which has been converted into a centre for heritage interpretation, makes a fitting end to the visit. Also in summer, you can watch an afternoon shooting demonstration, with a private and corporal in period dress firing off noisy rounds with gunpowder.

▼   The beautiful white roughcast Dauphine Redoubt. ©*Étienne Boucher*

The newest of Québec City's gates, **Porte Saint-Jean** actually has ancient origins. In 1693 it was one of only three entrances to the city. It was reinforced by Chaussegros de Léry in 1757, and then rebuilt by the British. To satisfy merchants who were clamouring for the total destruction of the walls, a "modern" gate equipped with tandem carriage tunnels and corresponding pedestrian passageways was erected in 1867. However, this structure did not fit in with Lord Dufferin's romantic vision of the city and was demolished in 1898. The present gate did not replace it until 1936.

At nº 29 Rue D'Auteuil is a former **Anglican Orphanage** built for the Society for Promoting Christian Knowledge in 1824. It was the first Gothic Revival style building in Québec City. Its architecture was portentous, as it inaugurated the romantic current that would eventually permeate the city. As you pass by, notice the two busts unveiled in 2004 in memory of Émile Nelligan and Alexander Pushkin by the cities of Québec and St. Petersburg, opposite no. 57 in **Parc de l'Esplanade**.

The last of Québec's Jesuits died in 1800, his community having been banished by the British and then, in 1774, by the Pope himself. The community was revived in 1814, however, and returned to Québec City in 1840. Since its college and church on Place de l'Hôtel-de-Ville were no longer available, they were welcomed by the Congregationists, a brotherhood founded by the Jesuit Ponert in 1657 with a view to propagating the cult of the Virgin. This group built the **Chapelle des Jésuites**. François Baillairgé designed the plans for the church, which was completed in 1818. The facade was redone in 1930. The decoration of the interior began with the construction of the counterfeit vaulting. Its centrepiece is Pierre-Noël Levasseur's altar (1770). Since 1925, the Jesuit church has been Québec's sanctuary for the veneration of the Canadian Martyrs.

Porte Kent, like Porte Saint-Louis, is the result of Lord Dufferin's romantic vision of the city. The plans for this gate, Vieux-Québec's prettiest, were drawn up in 1878 by Charles Baillairgé, following the suggestions of Irishman William H. Lynn.

▲   The Chapelle des Jésuites. ©Philippe Renault/Hemis

▶   The Porte Saint-Jean gateway. ©Société du 400ᵉ anniversaire de Québec

On the other side of the walls stands the Hôtel du Parlement and inside, several patrician homes along the Rue D'Auteuil. Number 69, **Maison McGreevy**, stands out by its sheer size. The house is the work of Thomas Fuller, the architect of the Parliament Buildings in Ottawa and New York's State Capitol. It was built in 1868 by McGreevy, a construction entrepreneur who also built Canada's first parliament buildings. Behind the rather commercial-looking facade of yellow Nepean sandstone is a perfectly preserved Victorian interior.

Vieux-Québec

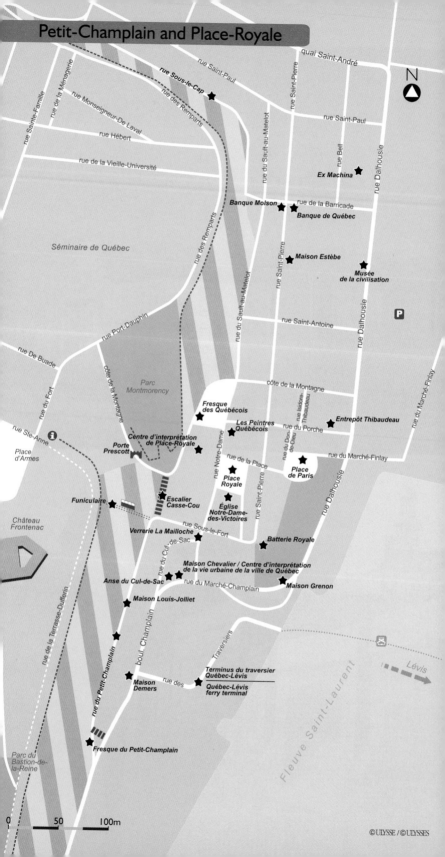

Petit-Champlain and Place-Royale

quai Saint-André

rue Saint-Paul

rue Sous-le-Cap

rue des Remparts

rue Monseigneur-De Laval

rue de la Ménagerie

rue Sainte-Famille

rue Hébert

rue de la Vieille-Université

rue Sault-au-Matelot

rue Saint-Pierre

rue Saint-Paul

rue Bell

rue Dalhousie

Ex Machina

rue de la Barricade

Banque Molson

Banque de Québec

Séminaire de Québec

rue des Remparts

Maison Estèbe

rue Saint-Pierre

Musée de la civilisation

rue du Sault-au-Matelot

rue Port-Dauphin

rue Saint-Antoine

P

rue De Buade

côte de la Montagne

côte de la Montagne

Parc Montmorency

rue du Don-de-Dieu

rue Isidore-Thibaudeau

rue du Marché-Finlay

rue Ste-Anne

Fresque des Québécois

Les Peintres Québécois

rue du Porche

Entrepôt Thibaudeau

Place d'Armes

Porte Prescott

Centre d'interprétation de Place-Royale

rue Notre-Dame

rue de la Place

Place de Paris

rue du Marché-Finlay

Funiculaire

Escalier Casse-Cou

Place Royale

rue Saint-Pierre

rue Dalhousie

Château Frontenac

Verrerie La Mailloche

rue Sous-le-Fort

Église Notre-Dame-des-Victoires

Batterie Royale

rue du Cul-de-Sac

Maison Chevalier / Centre d'interprétation de la vie urbaine de la ville de Québec

Anse du Cul-de-Sac

rue du Marché-Champlain

Maison Grenon

Maison Louis-Jolliet

boul. Champlain

rue de la Terrasse-Dufferin

rue du Petit-Champlain

Traversiers

Lévis

Maison Demers

rue des

Terminus du traversier Québec-Lévis

Québec-Lévis ferry terminal

Fleuve Saint-Laurent

Parc du Bastion-de-la-Reine

Fresque du Petit-Champlain

0   50   100m

©ULYSSE / ©ULYSSES

Petit-Champlain and Place-Royale

The historic, ever-popular Petit-Champlain neighbour-hood, whose namesake street hosts a theatre, cafés, restaurants, studios, galleries and boutiques, is unparal-leled for relaxing, people-watching and meeting with friends. Several well-known artists and artisans have set up shop here.

The Place-Royale area is the most European quarter of any city in North America, resembling a village in north-western France. Place-Royale is laden with symbolism, as it was on this very spot that New France was founded in 1608. After many unsuccessful attempts, this became the official departure point of French exploits in America. Under the French Regime, Place-Royale was the only densely populated area in a vast, untamed colony. Today, it contains the most significant concentration of 17th- and 18th-century buildings in the Americas north of Mexico.

PETIT-CHAMPLAIN

The **Funiculaire** (Funicular) began operating in November 1879. It was installed by entrepreneur W. A. Griffith in order to link the lower and upper towns. When the funicular was first built, water was transferred from one reservoir to another to make it function. It was converted to electricity in 1906, at the same time that Terrasse Dufferin was illuminated. The funicular is an outdoor elevator that eliminates the need to take the *Escalier Casse-Cou*, or "break-neck stairway," or to go around Côte de la Montagne.

Porte Prescott can be reached from Côte de la Montagne or from Terrasse Dufferin by means of a stairway and a charming footbridge located near the funicular's entryway. This discreetly postmodern structure, built in 1983, sought to evoke the 1797 gate by Gother Mann. It allows pedestrians to cross directly from Terrasse Dufferin to Parc Montmorency.

The **Escalier Casse-Cou**, which literally means "break-neck strairway," has been here since 1682. Until the beginning of the 20th century, it had been made of planks that were in constant need of repair or replacement. It connects the various businesses situated on different levels.

Among these is a small *économusée* (economuseum) which unveils the secrets of glass-blowing. At **Verrerie La Mailloche**, visitors can observe the fascinating spectacle of artisans shaping molten

▼ View of Petit-Champlain from an Escalier Casse-Cou terrace. ©Denis Vincelette

glass according to traditional techniques. The finished products are sold in a shop on the second floor.

At the foot of the stairway is **Rue du Petit-Champlain**, once inhabited by the Irish who worked in the city's port and refered to the street as "Little Champlain Street." Today, this narrow pedestrian street is flanked by charming craft shops and pleasant cafés located in 17th- and 18th-century houses. Some of the houses at the foot of the cape were destroyed by rockslides before the cliff was reinforced during the 19th century.

Maison Louis-Jolliet at 16 Rue du Petit-Champlain was one of the earliest houses in Vieux-Québec (1683) and one of the few works by Claude Baillif still standing. The house was built after the great fire of 1682, which destroyed Basse-Ville. It was this tragedy that prompted the authorities to require that stone be used in all buildings. Louis Jolliet (1645-1700) was the man who, along with Father Marquette, discovered the Mississippi and explored Hudson Bay. During the last years of his life, he taught hydrography at the Séminaire de Québec. The interior of the house was completely gutted and now contains the lower platform of the funicular.

You will probably need a few minutes to admire the many details that make up the beautiful **Fresque du Petit-Champlain**. Some 35 characters, both famous and obscure, who shaped the history of the province of Québec, and most particularly of Québec City and the Petit-Champlain district, come to life in six rooms. From the first floor to the attic, they are presented in various settings, such as artisan workshops and an inn. You'll feel as though the walls have suddenly opened up to reveal different chapters in history!

Maison Demers was built in 1689 by mason Jean Lerouge. This impressive residence is an example of the bourgeois style of Québec City's Basse-Ville. A two-

▲   The Fresque du Petit-Champlain.
©Louise Leblanc

storey residential facade looks onto Rue du Petit-Champlain while the rear, which was used as a warehouse, extends down another two storeys to open directly onto the Anse du Cul-de-Sac.

The cove called **Anse du Cul-de-Sac**, also known as Anse aux Barques, was Québec City's first port. In 1745, Intendant Gilles Hocquart ordered the construction of a major shipyard in the western part of the cove. Several French battleships were built there using Canadian lumber.

In 1854, the terminus of the Grand Trunk railway was built on the embankments, and in 1858 the Marché Champlain went up, only to be destroyed by fire in 1899. The location is presently occupied by

Petit-Champlain and Place-Royale

administrative buildings and by the **terminal of the Québec-Lévis ferry**. A short return trip on the ferry provides a spectacular view of Vieux-Québec as a whole. Taking the ferry in the winter affords a rare chance to come face to face with the ice floes on the St. Lawrence River.

If the weather is threatening, you can still enjoy the magnificent view of the St. Lawrence and the city of Lévis on the opposite bank by stepping inside the ferry terminal, whose large glass windows look out onto this splendid natural scene.

Hôtel Jean-Baptiste-Chevalier, a former hotel, was the first building in the area to be restored. The hotel is really three separate houses from three different periods: **Maison de l'Armateur Chevalier** (home of Chevalier the shipowner), built in a square in 1752; **Maison Frérot**, with a mansard roof (1683); and **Maison Dolbec**, dating from 1713. These houses were all repaired or partially rebuilt after the British Conquest. As a group, they were rescued from deterioration in 1955 by Gérard Morisset, the director of the province's Inventaire des Œuvres d'Art, who suggested that they be purchased and restored by the government of Québec. This decision had a domino effect that prevented the demolition of the sector.

Maison Chevalier houses an annex of the Musée de la Civilisation: the **Centre d'Interprétation de la Vie Urbaine de la Ville de Québec**, an information centre on urban life in Québec City. This centre offers walking tours of the city and other educational activities.

The early 18th-century classical French Maison Chevalier is a fine example of urban architecture in New France. The exhibit *A Sense of the Past (Ambiances d'autrefois)* explains the history of the

Petit-Champlain and Place-Royale

▶ The Fresque des Québécois (see p 79) pays homage to the city's founders and builders.
©Philippe Renault/Hemis

building and shows 18th- and 19th-century interiors recreated using pieces from the collection of the Musée de la Civilisation.

Before you reach the Batterie Royale, cross the small Passage de la Batterie which leads to **Maison Grenon** (1763). The house's pretty courtyard offers a great view of the Château Frontenac and the ferries crossing the river.

With no walls to protect the Basse-Ville, other means of defending it from the cannon-fire of ships in the river had to be found. Following the attack by Admiral Phips in 1690, it was decided to set up the **Batterie Royale** at the far end of modern-day Rue Sous-le-Fort, according to a plan drawn up by Claude Baillif. The strategic position of the battery allowed for the bombardment of any enemy ships

foolhardy enough to venture into the narrows in front of the city. The ruins of the battery, long hidden under storehouses, were discovered in 1974. The crenellations, removed in the 19th century, were reconstructed, as was the wooden portal, shown in a sketch from 1699.

The two rough stone houses on Rue Saint-Pierre, next to the battery, were built for Charles Guillemin in the early 18th century. The narrowness of the house on the left shows just how precious land was in the Basse-Ville during the French regime. Each lot, no matter how irregular, had to be used. A little further along, at 25 Rue Saint-Pierre, is the **Maison Fornel**, where a number of artifacts are on display in a vaulted basement, which was built in the 17th century from the ruins of Champlain's stronghold and extends right under the square.

◄ The Québec-Lévis ferry with the Basse-Ville in the background. ©Istockphoto.com/Tony Tremblay

▼ The unique Maison Chevalier. ©Jacques Lessard

Québec's port and commercial area is a narrow U-shaped piece of land wedged between Cap Diamant and the waters of the St. Lawrence River. This area is called the Basse-Ville of Vieux-Québec because of its location at the foot of the Cap Diamant escarpment. The cradle of New France, the Place-Royale neighbourhood is where Samuel de Champlain (1567-1635) founded the settlement he called the "Abitation" in 1608, which would eventually become Québec City. In the summer of 1759, three quarters of the city was badly damaged by British bombardment. It took 20 years to repair and rebuild the houses.

In the 19th century, the construction of multiple embankments allowed the expansion of the town and enabled the area around Place Royale to be linked by road with the area around the intendant's palace. The port's decline at the beginning of the 20th century led to the gradual abandonment of Place-Royale; restoration work began in 1959.

PLACE-ROYALE

Place-Royale's 27 vaulted cellars are among the oldest and most beautiful in Québec City, and make up a large share of the approximately 65 residential vaulted cellars in the whole city. Most of these were constructed in the 17th century under the French regime.

The square itself was laid out in 1673 by Governor Frontenac as a market. It replaced the garden of Champlain's Abitation, a stronghold that went up in flames in 1682 along with the rest of Basse-Ville. In 1686, Intendant Jean Bochart de Champigny erected a **bronze bust of Louis XIV** in the middle of the square, hence the

VAULTED CELLARS

Today, some 65 residential vaulted cellars remain in Québec City. Most were constructed during the 18th century under the French regime. Some of the 27 vaulted cellars in the Place-Royale area in the Basse-Ville have survived in good repair and are now open to the public (including those of Maison Chevalier, Maison Pagé-Quercy, Maison Estèbe, part of the Musée de la Civilisation, and Maison Fornel).

Besides protecting the house from the dampness of the cellar and reinforcing the ground floor, these stone cellars protected against theft, fire, and even bombardment. But above all, they served as cold rooms offering a temperature of about 15°C and a constant humidity, useful for storing perishable goods such as fruits and vegetables, dairy products, salt fish, alcohol, vinegar, oil, salt pork, and other meats.

◀ The Maison Pagé-Quercy's vaulted cellar, in the Musée de la Civilisation. ©Idra Labrie

name of the square, **Place Royale**. In 1928, François Bokanowski, the French Minister of Commerce and Communications, presented Québec MNA Athanase David with a bronze replica of the marble bust of Louis XIV in the Gallerie de Diane at Versailles to replace the missing statue. The bronze, by Alexis Rudier, was not set up until 1931, for fear of offending Britain.

Small, unpretentious **Église Notre-Dame-des-Victoires** is the oldest church in Canada. Designed by Claude Baillif, it dates from 1688. It was built on the foundations of Champlain's *Abitation* and incorporates some of its walls. Beside the church, black granite marks the remains of the foundations of the second Abitation de Champlain. These vestiges were discovered in 1976.

Initially dedicated to the Child Jesus, it was rechristened Notre-Dame-de-la-Victoire after Admiral Phipps' 1690 attack failed. It was later renamed Notre-Dame-des-Victoires (the plural) in memory of the misfortune of British Admiral Walker, whose fleet ran aground on Île aux Œufs during a storm in 1711. The bombardments of the Conquest left nothing standing but the walls of the church, ruining Levasseur's lovely interior. The church was restored in 1766, but was not fully rebuilt until the current steeple was added in 1861.

Raphaël Giroux is responsible for most of the present interior, which was undertaken between 1854 and 1857, but the strange "fortress" tabernacle of the main altar is a later work by David Ouellet (1878). Lastly, in 1888, Jean Tardivel painted the historical scenes on the vault and on the wall of the chancel. Most striking, though, are the various artworks in the church: the *ex-voto* (an offering) that hangs from the centre of the vault depicting the *Brézé*, a ship that came to Canada in 1664 carrying soldiers of the Carignan Regiment; and the beautiful tabernacle in the Sainte-Geneviève chapel, attributed to Pierre-Noël Levasseur (circa 1730). Among the paintings are works by Boyermans and Van Loo, originally from the collection of Abbé Desjardins.

Under the French Regime, the square attracted many merchants and ship owners who commissioned the building of attractive residences. The tall house on the southwest corner of the square and on Rue de la Place, **Maison Barbel**, was built in 1754 for the formidable businesswoman Anne-Marie Barbel, widow of Louis Fornel. At the time, she owned a pottery factory on the Rivière Saint-Charles and held the lease on the lucrative trading post at Tadoussac.

Maison Dumont, at 1 Place Royale, was designed in 1689 for vintner Eustache Lambert Dumont. The house incorporated parts of the old store of the Compagnie des Habitants (1647). Visitors can see its huge vaulted basement, still used, as it was in the past, to store casks and bottles of wine. Turned into an inn in the 19th century, the house was a favourite stopover for U.S. President William Howard Taft (1857-1930) on his way to his annual summer vacation in La Malbaie.

Maison Bruneau-Rageot-Drapeau, at number 3A, is a house built in 1763 using the walls of the old Nicolas Jérémie house. Jérémie was an Innu interpreter and a clerk at the fur-trading posts of Hudson Bay.

Maison Paradis, at 42 Rue Notre-Dame, houses **Les Peintres Québécois** art gallery. The gallery shows works by such important figures of the Québec art world as Clarence Gagnon and Jean-Paul Lemieux, as well as pieces by up-and-coming new artists.

▼ Place Royale, where Samuel de Champlain founded Québec City in 1608. ©istockphoto.com/Tony Tremblay

S-SHAPED LINCHPINS

You have perhaps noticed the S-shaped pieces of iron that decorate the walls of some of this neighbourhood's old houses. These objects are linchpins that hold the stones in the walls on which the weight of the roof rests.

This reinforcement system helps to keep the walls straight; an S on the side of the outside of the building has a counterpart on the inside, connected by a long iron bolt that passes through the beams and therefore is not visible inside the house.

▶ Two S-shaped iron linchpins atop a facade.
©Dreamstime.com/Christopher Howey

On Rue Notre-Dame, near Côte de la Montagne, strollers can get a look at the blind wall of Maison Soumande, in front of Parc de La Cetière, and its **Fresque des Québécois**. Despite its brilliant colours, it's easy to miss – it's a spectacular example of *trompe l'œil*! Created by artists from France's Cité de la Création de Lyon in collaboration with SODEC and the Commission de la Capitale Nationale du Québec, the startlingly realistic mural required 600 litres of paint. On a surface area of 420m², the artists summed up Québec City's architecture and scenes such as Cap Diamant, the ramparts, a bookshop, houses of Vieux-Québec—in short, the places that the town's inhabitants see every day. Just like the crowd of admiring onlookers that appears rain or shine, you're sure to spend a few minutes identifying the historical figures and the role they played. From top to bottom and from left to right, you will see Marie Guyart, Catherine de Longpré, François-Xavier Garneau, Louis-Joseph Papineau, Jean Talon, the Comte de Frontenac, Marie Fitzbach, Marcelle Mallet, Louis Jolliet, Alphonse Desjardins, Lord Dufferin, Félix Leclerc and finally Samuel de Champlain, who started it all.

Petit-Champlain and Place-Royale

Return to Place Royale and visit the **Centre d'Interprétation de Place-Royale**. To accommodate the centre, both the Hazeur and Smith houses, which had burned down, were rebuilt in a modern style using a large portion of the original materials. The omnipresent glass walls show off the exhibits and architecture from all angles. Several fun and instructive exhibits for children and grownups are available; activities such as a period costume workshop and guided tours reveal the 400-year history of one of North America's oldest neighbourhoods.

Along the glass walls between the two houses of the interpretive centre, a stairway goes down Côte de la Montagne to Place Royale. From the staircase, you can see some of the centre's treasures. On each of the three levels, an exhibition presents chapters of Place-Royale's history. There are also artifacts discovered during archaeological digs under the square. Whether they are whole objects or tiny fragments that are difficult to identify, they are all instructive.

You can also watch a multimedia show and admire various scale models, such as the one representing the second Abitation of Champlain in 1635. You will learn, among other things, that Québec City's first hotel was opened in 1648 by the appropriately named Sieur Boidon (*bois donc* means "have a drink!"). The hotel tradition continued on Place Royale until the middle of the 20th century, when the last hotel was destroyed by fire. A film and models tell the adventures of Samuel de Champlain, allowing visitors to trace his footsteps into the New World.

Place de Paris, bordering Rue du Marché-Finlay, is an elegant and sophisticated combination of contemporary art and traditional surroundings designed by Québécois architect Jean Jobin in 1987. A large sculpture by French artist Jean-Pierre Raynault dominates the centre of the square. The work was presented to the city by Jacques Chirac, then mayor of Paris, on behalf of his city. Entitled *Dialogue avec l'Histoire* (Dialogue with History), the black granite and white marble work with lighting elements evokes the earliest human presence in the area and forms a pair with the bust of Louis XIV visible in the background. The locals have dubbed it the Colossus of Québec because of its imposing dimensions. From the square, which was once a market, there is a splendid view of the Batterie Royale and the St. Lawrence River.

Entrepôt Thibaudeau, also on Rue du Marché-Finlay, is a huge building whose stone facade faces Rue Dalhousie. It represents the last prosperous days of the area before its decline at the end of the 19th century. The Second Empire building is distinguished by its mansard roof and by its segmental arch openings. It was built in 1880, following the plans of Joseph-Ferdinand Peachy, for Isidore Thibaudeau, president and founder of the Banque Nationale and importer of European novelties.

Further along at number 92 is yet another imposing merchant's house, **Maison Estèbe** (1752). It is now part of the Musée de la Civilisation, whose smooth stone walls face Rue Saint-Pierre. Guillaume Estèbe was a businessman and the director of the Saint-Maurice ironworks in Trois-Rivières. Having participated in a number of unsavoury schemes with Intendant Bigot during the Seven Years' War, he was locked up in the Bastille for a few months on embezzlement charges. The house where he lived for five years with his wife and 14 children is built

Petit-Champlain and Place-Royale

▶   The famous Maison Estèbe. ©*Pierre Soulard*

on an embankment that used to face a large private wharf, now the courtyard of the museum. The courtyard is accessible through the nearby gateway. The 21-room interior escaped the bombardments of 1759. Some of the rooms feature handsome Louis XV woodwork.

At the corner of Rue de la Barricade is the old **Banque de Québec** building (1861). Across the street, the old **Banque Molson** occupies an 18th-century house.

The **Musée de la Civilisation** is housed in a building that was completed in 1988 in the traditional architectural style of Québec City, with its stylized roof, dormer windows and a belltower like those common to the area. Architect Moshe Safdie, who also designed the revolutionary Habitat 67 in Montréal and Ottawa's National Gallery, designed a sculptural building with a monumental exterior staircase at its centre. The lobby provides a charming view of Maison Estèbe and its wharf while preserving a contemporary look underlined by Astri Reusch's sculpture, *La Débâcle*.

The Musée de la Civilisation presents a great variety of temporary exhibitions. Themes such as humour, circus and song,

for example, have been the object of very lively displays. Travelling exhibitions also recount the world's great civilizations, while permanent exhibitions provide a portrait of the local culture.

Le Temps des Québécois recounts the history of the Québec people; *Nous, les Premières Nations*, developed in collaboration with First Nations peoples, is a large exhibition tracing the history of the 11 Aboriginal nations of Québec. You can view many objects as well as audiovisual materials, some the work of filmmaker Arthur Lamothe. The most recent permanent exhibit, *Territoires*, deals with broad themes such as land use (*Un Territoire Habité*), natural resources (*Un Territoire de Ressources*), the discovery of nature (*Un Territoire de Loisirs*), and adapting to Québec's harsh winter (*Un Territoire Nordique*).

Some of the more remarkable items are the Aboriginal artifacts, the large French Regime fishing craft unearthed during excavations for the museum itself, some highly ornate 19th-century horse-drawn hearses, and some Chinese *objets d'art* and pieces of furniture, including an imperial bed, from the collection of the Jesuits. You can also visit the museum's vaulted cellar, which dates from the 18th century.

▼ Inside the Musée de la Civilisation.
©Philippe Renault/Hemis

Beside the Musée de la Civilisation is a lavish Beaux-Arts fire station dating from 1912 that now houses **Ex Machina**, a multi-disciplinary artistic production centre founded by Robert Lepage. Note the high tower with a copper dome rising on the southeast corner like a church spire, which was inspired by the tower of the Hôtel du Parlement. Firefighters used to hang the fabric hoses of the day in the tower to dry and prevent rotting. The building has been expanded, and in order to preserve its character, a false

▲ Ex Machina, an arts centre founded by theatre director Robert Lepage. ©Vanessa Landry Claverie

wall similar to the original stone wall—but made of plastic—has been erected in front of the new section. This section is topped with a small glass and metal sculpture that lights up at night. A glass case holds statuettes representing the numerous awards won by Robert Lepage both at home and abroad for his work in theatre and film.

Petit-Champlain and Place-Royale

Vieux-Port

N

Fleuve Saint-Laurent

© ULYSSE / © ULYSSES

★ Pointe-à-Carcy

★ Musée naval de Québec
Naval Museum of Québec

Édifice de la Douane

rue Dalhousie

★ Banque canadienne
de commerce
Canadian Imperial Bank of Commerce

rue Bell

rue St-Pierre

rue Dalhousie

★ Centre d'interprétation
du Vieux-Port-de-Québec
Old Port of Québec
Interpretation Centre

★ Place de la FAO

rue du Sault-
au-Matelot

rue Sous-le-Cap

rue des Remparts

rue Hébert

quai Saint-André

★ rue Saint-Paul

rue
Sainte-Famille

rue Ferland

rue Saint-Flavien

Bassin Louise

rue Hamel

rue des Remparts

rue Charlevoix

Basse-Ville

Rivière Saint-Charles

rue de l'Estuaire

rue Abraham-Martin

★ Marché du Vieux-Port

H

rue Abraham-Martin

quai Saint-André

★ Gare du Palais

rue de l'Estuaire

★ Place de la Gare

★ Ancien bureau de poste
post office

★ Îlot Saint-Nicolas /
Maisons Lecourt

rue De Saint-Vallier

Quartier du Palais

rue de la Gare-du-Palais

Parc de l'Artillerie

★ Parc
de l'Amérique-Latine

rue Saint-Nicolas

★ Cabaret
Chez Gérard

★ L'îlot des Palais

rue Vallière

boul. Jean-Lesage

boul. Jean-Lesage

boul. Charest E.

rue des Prairies

Parc Tessier

440

440

0   75   150m

Vieux-Port

The Vieux-Port (old port) is often criticized for being overly North American in a city with such a pronounced European sensibility. It was first refurbished by the Canadian government as part of the maritime celebration *Québec 1534-1984*, and once again for Québec City's 400th anniversary celebrations.

With its dome and columns, the handsome **Édifice de la Douane** (customs house), at 2 Quai St-André, features lovely neoclassical architecture. At the time the structure was built (1856-1857), the river actually flowed right next to it.

The area between Rue Dalhousie and the river is called **Pointe-à-Carcy**. It includes Quais 19, 21, and 22.

The **Naval Museum of Québec** was opened in May 1995 and named in honour of Lt.-Cdr. Joseph Alexis Stanislas Déry, a Second World War veteran. This museum, located where the Bassin Louise meets the St. Lawrence, is part of the Pointe-à-Carcy Naval Complex, which includes the old port's Canadian Forces Naval Reserve buildings. Its permanent exhibition is devoted to the naval history of the St. Lawrence River, but also to the values of peace. Outside, the end of the pier offers an excellent view of the river and ships.

Place de la FAO is located at the intersection of Rue Saint-Pierre, Rue Saint-Paul and Rue Sault-au-Matelot. This square honours the United Nations Food and Agriculture Organisation, whose first meeting was held at the Château Frontenac in 1945. The sculpture at the centre of the square, *La Vivrière*, represents the prow of a ship as it emerges from the waves, its female figurehead firmly grasping all kinds of fruit, vegetables and grains.

In the square at the corner of Rue Saint-Pierre stands an imposing building with a large round portico which formerly housed the **Canadian Imperial Bank of Commerce**.

Rue de la Barricade leads to **Rue Sous-le-Cap**. This narrow pedestrian passage was once wedged between the St. Lawrence River and the Cap Diamant escarpment. At the end of the 19th century, the

▲ Place de la FAO and its *La Vivrière* sculpture.
©Philippe Renault/Hemis

▶ Rue Sous-le-Cap, a narrow pedestrian passage. ©Patrick Donovan

street housed working-class families of Irish origin. Today's inhabitants, finding the houses too small, have renovated the little cottages on the side of the cliff and connected them to their houses by walkways crossing the street at clothesline height. One almost enters Rue Sous-le-Cap on tiptoe because of the feeling of walking into another world. At the end of the street is Côte du Colonel-Dambourgès and then Rue Saint-Paul.

Vieux-Port

Rue Saint-Paul is a most pleasant street, lined with antique shops and art galleries that overflow with beautiful Québec heritage furniture, as well as a few quality restaurants.

In the days of sailboats, Québec City was one of the most important gateways to North America, since many vessels could not make their way any farther against the current. Its bustling port was surrounded by shipyards that made great use of the plentiful and high-quality Canadian lumber. The first royal shipyards appeared under the French regime in the cove known as Anse du Cul-de-Sac. The Napoleonic blockade of 1806 forced the British to turn to their Canadian colony for wood and for the construction of battleships. This was a great boost for a number of shipyards and made fortunes for many of their owners. The **Old Port of Québec Interpretation Centre** is a national historic site that concentrates on those flourishing days of navigation in Québec.

Most of Québec City's public markets were shut down in the 1960s because they had become obsolete with the advent of supermarkets. However, people continued to yearn for fruit and vegetables fresh from the farm as well as the contact with the farmers. The markets gradually began to reappear at the beginning of the 1980s. **Marché du Vieux-Port**, at the corner of Rue Saint-Thomas and Quai St-André, was built in 1987 by architectural

▼ Rue Saint-Paul, lined with art galleries and antique shops. ©Philippe Renault/Hemis

partners Belzile, Brassard, Galienne and Lavoie. It is the successor to two other markets, Finlay and Champlain, that no longer exist. In the summer, the market is a pleasant place to stroll and take in the view of the Marina Bassin Louise at the edge of the market.

For over 50 years, the citizens of Québec City clamoured for a train station worthy of their city. Canadian Pacific finally fulfilled their wish in 1915. Designed by New York architect Harry Edward Prindle in the same style as the Château Frontenac, the superb **Gare du Palais** gives visitors a taste of the romance and charm that await them in Québec City. The 18m-high arrival hall that extends behind the giant window of the facade is bathed in sunlight from the leaded glass skylight on the roof. The faience tiles and multicoloured bricks in the walls lend a striking aspect to the entire ambiance.

The station was closed for almost 10 years (from 1976 to 1985) at the time when railway companies were imitating airlines and moving their stations to the suburbs. Fortunately, it was reopened with great pomp, and now houses the bus and train

stations. Across from it, **Place de la Gare-du-Palais** offers a lovely spot where you can relax and admire the impressive *Éclatement II*, a sculpture fountain designed by Charles Daudelin.

The neighbouring building is Raoul Chênevert's 1938 **post office**. It illustrates the persistence of the Château style of architecture that is so emblematic of the city.

A little further on Boulevard Jean-Lesage is **Parc de l'Amérique-Latine**. There, five monuments honour the memory of some of the most important figures in Latin American history: Juan Montalvo, José Gervasio Artigas, Bernado O'Higgings, Simón Bolívar and José Martí.

The heart of the **Quartier du Palais**, so named because it surrounds the former site of the Palais de l'Intendant, can be reached by heading west on Rue De Saint-Vallier.

The block bordered by Ruelle de l'Ancien-Chantier, Rue De Saint-Vallier, Rue Saint-Paul and Rue Saint-Nicolas is known as **Îlot Saint-Nicolas**. It was restored

▼   Québec City's old port ©*Tony Tremblay*

with verve by architects De Blois, Côté, Leahy. The handsome stone building on the corner and the two others behind it on Rue Saint-Nicolas housed the famous **Cabaret Chez Gérard** from 1938 to 1978. It was here that Charles Trenet, Rina Ketty and many other famous French singers performed. Charles Aznavour actually got his start here. In the bohemian days of the 1950s, he sang here every night for months for a mere pittance.

The big Scottish-brick building with the pinnacle inscribed "**Maisons Lecourt**" was erected across from l'Îlot Saint-Nicolas using the remnants of Intendant Bigot's "royal store." Nicknamed *La Friponne* (The Rogue's) because of the extortionary prices Bigot and his accomplices exacted from the miserable populace, the location was one of only two in the city during the French Regime where one could moor a boat (the other being Anse du Cul-de-Sac). In the 17th century, warehouses and wharfs were built along the estuary of the Saint-Charles, as was a shipyard with a dry dock that bequeathed the street its name, Rue de l'Ancien-Chantier, meaning "old shipyard."

The intendant oversaw the day-to-day affairs of the colony, and the royal stores, the few state enterprises and the prison were all located near his palace. With so many opportunities to enrich himself, it was only natural that his should be the most splendid mansion in New France. The remains of one wing of the palace can still be seen in the shape of the segment of brown brick foundation wall that is still visible. The location was originally the site of the brewery that was set up by the first intendant, Jean Talon (1625-1694). Talon took great effort to populate and develop the colony. For his trouble, he was made secretary of the king's cabinet upon his return to France. His brewery was replaced by a palace designed by engineer La Guer Morville in 1716. This

elegant building had a classical cut-stone entrance that led to a horseshoe-shaped staircase. Twenty or so ceremonial rooms were used for receptions and the meetings of the Conseil Supérieur.

▲ The Place de la Gare-du-Palais, with the train station in the background. ©Philippe Renault/Hemis

The palace was spared British cannon fire only to be burned to the ground during the American invasion of 1775-76. The arches of its cellars were used as the foundation of the Boswell brewery in 1872, bringing the site full circle. Today, the site hosts **L'Îlot des Palais**, which includes an archeological interpretation centre.

Vieux-Port

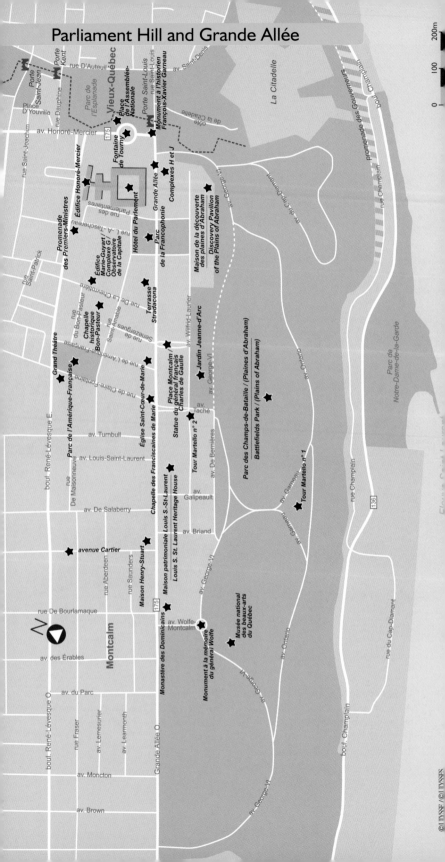

Parliament Hill and Grande Allée

200m

100

0

Porte Kent

rue D'Auteuil

Porte Saint-Jean

Porte Dauphine

Place D'Youville

rue Saint-Louis

rue Saint-Denis

La Citadelle

Vieux-Québec

Parc de l'Esplanade

Place de l'Assemblée-Nationale

Porte Saint-Louis

Monument à l'historien François-Xavier Garneau

côte de la Citadelle

promenade des Gouverneurs

boul. Champlain

av. Honoré-Mercier

rue Saint-Joachim

rue Dauphine

Fontaine de Tourny

175

Grande Allée

Complexes H et J

av. Georges-VI

rue Champlain

Édifice Honoré-Mercier

Promenade des Premiers-Ministres

rue des Parlementaires

Hôtel du Parlement

Parc de la Francophonie

Maison de la découverte des plaines d'Abraham / Discovery Pavilion of the Plains of Abraham

rue Saint-Patrick

Édifice Marie-Guyart / Complexe G / Observatoire de la Capitale

rue L.-A.-Taschereau

rue De La Chevrotière

Terrasse Stadacona

Grand Théâtre

Chapelle historique Bon-Pasteur

du Bon-Pasteur

rue Saint-Amable

rue Scott

rue de l'Amérique-Française

av. Wilfrid-Laurier

av. George-VI

Jardin Jeanne-d'Arc

Parc de l'Amérique-Française

rue De Claire-Fontaine

Église Saint-Cœur-de-Marie

rue De La Chevrotière

Place Montcalm / général Français Charles de Gaulle

Statue du général Français

av. Taché

boul. René-Lévesque E.

av. Turnbull

rue De Maisonneuve

av. Louis-Saint-Laurent

Chapelle des Franciscaines de Marie

Tour Martello n° 2

av. De Bernières

Parc des Champs-de-Bataille / (Plaines d'Abraham)
Battlefields Park / Plains of Abraham

av. De Salaberry

av. Galipeault

av. Briand

Tour Martello n° 1

av. Garneau

av. Ontario

rue Champlain

136

avenue Cartier

Maison patrimoniale Louis-S.-St-Laurent
Louis S. St. Laurent Heritage House

rue Aberdeen

rue Saunders

Maison Henry-Stuart

av. George-VI

175

rue De Bourlamaque

av. Wolfe-Montcalm

Monastère des Dominicains

Musée national des beaux-arts du Québec

av. Ontario

rue du Cap-Diamant

N

Montcalm

av. des Érables

Monument à la mémoire du général Wolfe

av. du Parc

Grande Allée O.

boul. René-Lévesque O.

rue Fraser

rue Lemesurier

av. Moncton

av. Brown

av. George-VI

boul. Champlain

Parliament Hill and Grande Allée

The various buildings of the parliamentary precinct, known in French as the Colline Parlementaire ("parliament hill"), are the workplaces of thousands of civil servants. The area's attractive layout also draws tourists with its architecture and landscaping.

Just outside the city walls, the magnificent Grande Allée is one of the attractive roads leading into Vieux-Québec. It hosts several of the capital's government departments, but this bureaucratic function does not detract from its lively character day and night. The elegant old houses on its eastern end host lively new cafés, restaurants and nightclubs for all tastes, budgets and ages.

▲ The Hôtel du Parlement, the seat of the government of Québec. ©iStockPhoto.com/Tony Tremblay

PARLIAMENT HILL

Near Porte Saint-Louis stands Paul Chevré's **monument to historian François-Xavier Garneau** and the **Croix du Sacrifice**, where Remembrance Day services are held every year on November 11.

The **Hôtel du Parlement** is better known to the Québécois as the Assemblée Nationale or National Assembly, which strictly speaking is the name of the provincial legislature it houses. The seat of the government of Québec, this imposing building was erected between 1877 and 1886. It has a lavish French Renaissance

Parliament Hill

Revival exterior intended to reflect the unique cultural status of Québec in the North American context. Eugène-Étienne Taché (1836-1912) looked to the Louvre for inspiration for both the plan of the quadrangular building and its decor. It was originally designed to house a bicameral parliament typical of the British system of government, as well as all of the ministries; today, like all of Canada's provinces, Québec's legislature has only one house, while the ministries have expanded into a group of buildings on either side of Grande Allée.

Parliament Hill

The numerous statues on the parliament's main facade constitute a sort of pantheon of Québec. The 22 bronzes of important figures in the history of Québec were cast by such well-known artists as Louis-Philippe Hébert and Alfred Laliberté. A raised inscription on the wall near the central passage identifies the statues. In front of the main entrance a bronze by Hébert entitled *La Halte dans la Forêt* (The Pause in the Forest) depicts an Aboriginal family. The work, which is meant to honour the original inhabitants of Québec, was displayed at the Paris World's Fair in 1889. *Le Pêcheur à la Nigog* (Fisherman at the Nigog), by the same artist, hangs in the niche by the fountain. The building's interior is a veritable compendium of the icons of Québec's history. The handsome woodwork is done in the tradition of religious architecture.

The members of the legislature, called *députés* or MNAs (Members of the National Assembly), sit in the National Assembly chamber or Salon Bleu (Blue Chamber), where Charles Huot's painting, *La Première Séance de l'Assemblée Législative du Bas-Canada en 1792* (The First Session of the Legislative Assembly of Lower Canada in 1792), hangs over the chair of the president of the Assembly. A large work by the same artist covers the ceiling and evokes the motto of Québec, *Je me souviens* (I remember). The Salon Rouge (Red Chamber), intended for the Conseil Législatif, an unelected body that was abolished in 1968, is now used for parliamentary commissions. A painting entitled *Le Conseil Souverain* (The Sovereign Council), a reminder of the style of government in the days of New France, graces this chamber.

Several of the windows of the parliament building boast gorgeous Art Nouveau stained glass by master glazier Henri Perdriau, a native of Saint-Pierre de Montélimar in Vendée, France. Undeniably, the most spectacular is the one that adorns the entrance to the elegant **Le Parlementaire** restaurant. This feature was designed by architect Omer Marchand in 1917. National Assembly debates are open to the public, but a pass is required.

▼   The Hôtel du Parlement's Salon Bleu. *©Philippe Renault/Hemis*

▲ A statue of Maurice Duplessis faces the Hôtel du Parlement. ©Philippe Renault/Hemis

Several important monuments can be found around the Hôtel du Parlement: among these are one in honour of Honoré Mercier, Premier of Québec from 1887 to 1891; another in honour of Maurice Duplessis, Premier during the *grande noirceur*, or "great darkness" (1936-1939 and 1944-1959); as well as one representing René Lévesque, who holds a special place in the hearts of the Québécois and was the Premier from 1976 to 1985. Also, the **Promenade des Premiers-Ministres** presents panels listing the Premiers who have led Québec since 1867.

In front of the Hôtel du Parlement you'll notice the beautiful **Place de l'Assemblée-Nationale**, divided in two by handsome Avenue Honoré-Mercier. The side along the wall hosts many events throughout the year.

The splendid **Fontaine de Tourny** was installed on July 3, 2007, Québec City's 399th anniversary. Rising above a circular basin, it presides over the roundabout at the centre of Avenue Honoré-Mercier, admired by drivers and pedestrians alike.

Created by the Barbezat foundry in France in 1854, the 7m-tall fountain is one of six created by sculptor Mathurin Moreau with decorations by animal sculptor Alexandre Lambert Léonard. Moreau won the gold medal at the 1855 World's Fair in Paris for his work. In 1857, the mayor of Bordeaux had one installed at each end of the Allées de Tourny, named for a marquis who served as the town's intendant under King Louis XV.

Nearly a century and a half later, in 2003, the well-known businessman Peter Simons discovered one of the two fountains being sold off in pieces at the

Parliament Hill

Saint-Ouen market. He snapped it up and donated it to the people of Québec City. As a result, we can now admire this magnificent work, whose base consists of four figures, three female and one male, representing rivers. These support the octagonal basin decorated with fish and sea motifs, in which four children representing fishing and seafaring support an upper basin topped with an ornamental vase. At night, the fountain is beautifully illuminated. The commemorative plaque features a quotation from author and Québec City native Marie Laberge.

The dizzying growth of the civil service during the Quiet Revolution of the 1960s compelled the government to construct several modern buildings to house its various ministries. A row of beautiful Second Empire houses was demolished to make way for **Complexes H and J**, on Grande Allée opposite the Hôtel du Parlement. Dubbed "the bunker" by the Québécois, the 1970 building used to house the Premier's office.

Since the spring of 2002, the offices of the Premier and the Conseil Exécutif have been located in the beautiful **Édifice Honoré-Mercier**, on Boulevard René-Lévesque Est adjacent to the Hôtel du Parlement. In fact, this is actually a homecoming since the building housed the Premier's offices up until 1972. The building was entirely renovated, before the move but the beauty of its architecture was preserved, including its marble features, plaster mouldings and woodwork. It was built between 1922 and 1925 according to the designs of the architect Chênevert.

Parliament Hill

▶ The splendid Fontaine de Tourny at night.
©Étienne Boucher

▲ The exhibit inside the Discovery Pavilion of the Plains of Abraham. *©Philippe Renault/Hemis*

▲ The Discovery Pavilion of the Plains of Abraham. *©Philippe Renault/Hemis*

The Battlefields Park Interpretation Centre is on Avenue Wilfrid-Laurier behind the complexes H and J, which border the Plains of Abraham. Housed in one of the Citadelle buildings, the **Discovery Pavilion of the Plains of Abraham** should please Québec City natives as much as visitors. The ground floor contains an entrance to the plains, a number of services and staff to answer questions about the Parc des Champs-de-Bataille, its history and the many activities that go on here. Visitors can see an exhibit about the Plains of Abraham, as well as *Odyssey*, a multimedia show. Various guided tours leave from here, one of which takes place aboard "Abraham's Bus"!

Parc de la Francophonie and **Complexe G**, which appears in the background, both occupy the site of the old Saint-Louis quarter, today almost entirely vanished. Parc de la Francophonie was laid out for open-air shows. It is commonly referred to as *Le Pigeonnier* (dovecote), in reference to the interesting concrete structure at its centre, based on an idea by landscape architects Schreiber and Williams in 1973.

GRANDE ALLÉE

Grande Allée appears on 17th-century maps, but it was not completed until the first half of the 19th century, when the city grew beyond its walls. Grande Allée originally was a country road linking the town to the Chemin du Roy, and then to Montréal. At that time, it was bordered by the large agricultural properties of the nobility and clergy of the French regime. After the British Conquest, many of the domains were turned into country estates by English merchants who set their manors well back from the road. The neoclassical town then spilled over into the area before the Victorian city had a chance to stamp the landscape with its distinctive style.

A little further to the west, the fabric of the old city is again in evidence. **Terrasse Stadacona**, at numbers 640 to 664, is a neoclassical row of English-style townhouses: the multiple houses share a common facade. These houses date from 1847 and have been converted into bars and restaurants with terraces sheltered by multitudes of parasols. Opposite, at numbers 661 to 695, is a group of Second Empire houses that dates from 1882, a period when Grande Allée was the most fashionable street in Québec City. These houses show the

▲ Bustling Grande Allée. ©Philippe Renault/Hemis

influence of the parliamentary buildings on the residential architecture of the area. Three other houses on Grande Allée are worth mentioning for the eclecticism of their facades: **Maison du Manufacturier de Chaussures W. A. Marsh**, at number 625, the house of a prominent shoe manufacturer, which was designed in 1899 by Toronto architect Charles John Gibson; **Maison Garneau-Meredith**, at numbers 600 to 614, from the same year; and **Maison William Price**, at number 575, a little Romeo-and-Juliet-style house which is, unfortunately, dwarfed by the **Hôtel Loews Le Concorde**. The revolving restaurant **L'Astral** of this hotel affords a magnificent view of Haute-Ville and the Plains of Abraham.

In little **Place Montcalm**, next to the hotel, is a statue commemorating the general's death on September 13, 1759, at the Battle of the Plains of Abraham. The **statue of French General Charles de Gaulle** (1890-1970), which faces away from Montcalm, created quite a controversy when it was erected in the spring of 1997.

Farther along, at the entrance to the Plains of Abraham, **Jardin Jeanne-d'Arc** boasts magnificent flowerbeds and a statue of Joan of Arc astride a spirited charger. A huge drinking-water reservoir is located under this part of the Plains of Abraham.

Behind the austere facade of the mother house of the Sœurs du Bon-Pasteur, a community devoted to the education of abandoned and delinquent girls, is the charming, Baroque Revival-style **Chapelle Historique Bon-Pasteur**. Designed by Charles Baillairgé in 1866, this tall, narrow chapel houses an authentic baroque tabernacle dating from 1730. Pierre-Noël Levasseur's masterpiece of New France carving is surrounded by devotional miniatures hung on pilasters by the nuns.

Grande Allée

Atop the 31 storeys of **Édifice Marie-Guyart** in **Complexe G**, the **Observatoire de la Capitale**, provides a splendid view of Québec City and its surrounding area. At 221m in altitude, it is the highest observation point in the city.

Called Parc Claire-Fontaine until 1985, the **Parc de l'Amérique-Française** was inaugurated by then-Premier René Lévesque just months before he was defeated by Robert Bourassa. The park's large trees are joined by a row of flagpoles flying Québec's fleur de lis flag.

The **Grand Théâtre** is located at the far end of the park. Inaugurated in 1971, this theatre designed by Polish architect Victor Prus was to be a meeting place for the members of Québec City's high society. There was quite a scandal, therefore, when Jordi Bonet's mural was unveiled and the assembled crowd read the lines from a poem by Claude Péloquin: *"Vous êtes pas tannés de mourir, bande de caves?"* (Aren't you idiots tired of dying?). The theatre has two halls (Louis-Fréchette and Octave-Crémazie) and presents Québec City's symphony orchestra concerts as well as theatre, dance and variety shows. The Salle Louis-Fréchette was completely renovated in 2007 to improve the lighting and sound system and to install comfortable new seats.

Église Saint-Cœur-de-Marie was built for the Eudists in 1919 and designed by Ludger Robitaille. It looks more martial than devotional with its bartizans, machicolations and towers. Its large archways are reminiscent of a Mediterranean fortress. Across the road is the most outlandish row of Second Empire houses still standing in Québec City, at 455-555 Grande Allée Est, the **Terrasse Frontenac**. The product of Joseph-Ferdinand Peachy's imagination (1895), its slender, fantastical spires look like something from a fairy tale.

The **Chapelle des Franciscaines de Marie** is the chapel of a community of nuns. They commissioned the Sanctuaire de l'Adoration Perpétuelle (Sanctuary of Perpetual Adoration) in 1901. This exuberant Baroque Revival chapel invites the faithful to prayer and celebrates the everlasting

◀ Inside Chapelle Historique Bon-Pasteur.
©Philippe Renault/Hemis

◀ Flowerbeds line the walkways of Jardin Jeanne-d'Arc. ©Étienne Boucher

JEAN PAUL RIOPELLE, A GIANT AMONG GIANTS

Jean Paul Riopelle was one of Québec's most renowned painters both at home and abroad. Many of the impressive number of paintings he created are exhibited throughout the world. A lyrical abstract painter, sculptor, and engraver, best known for his monumental canvases and his sculptural fountain *La Joute* (The Joust) (1969-1974) in Montréal, he marked and influenced the world of contemporary art. He was born in Montréal in 1923, and his career took off in the 1940s while he was a member of Paul-Émile Borduas's art movement Les Automatistes.

In 1948, he was a co-signatory of the artistic manifesto *Refus global*, which scandalized Québec society and laid the aesthetic foundations for the Quiet Revolution. He lived in Paris for several years but returned to the province of Québec during the last years of his life. He died on March 12, 2002, in his manor on Île aux Grues, on the south shore of the St. Lawrence River. For the last several years, the Musée National des Beaux-Arts du Québec has devoted one of its galleries entirely to him. Among others, its exhibit includes *L'Hommage à Rosa Luxemburg*, whose immense size mirrors the immense stature of its creator.

presence of God. It features a small columned cupola supported by angels and a sumptuous marble canopy.

Several handsome bourgeois houses dating from the early 20th century face the chapel. Among them, at numbers 433-435, is the residence of John Holt, the owner of the Holt Renfrew chain of department stores. Both this and the neighbouring house at number 425 are designed like Scottish manors. Undeniably the most elegant, in its mild Flemish and Oriental eclecticism, is the house of Judge P. A. Choquette, designed by architect Georges-Émile Tanguay.

At number 201, the first floor of the **Louis S. St. Laurent Heritage House** can be visited. Louis St. Laurent, prime minister of Canada from 1948 to 1957, had this house built in 1913 and lived there until his death in 1973. The exhibit shows the St. Laurent family and details the former prime minister's political life.

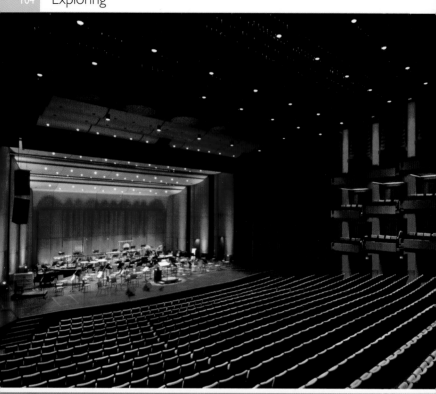

Maison Henry-Stuart, on the corner of Cartier and Grande Allée, is one of the few remaining Regency-style Anglo-Norman cottages in Québec City. This type of colonial British architecture is distinguished by a large pavilion roof overhanging a low veranda surrounding the building.

The house was built in 1849 and used to mark the border between the city and the country; its original garden still surrounds it. The interior features several pieces of furniture from the Saint-Jean-Port-Joli manor of Philippe Aubert de Gaspé, and has been practically untouched since 1911. Maison Henry-Stuart and its garden,

▲ The beautifully landscaped Maison Henry-Stuart. ©Conseil des monuments et sites du Québec

◄ The Grand Théâtre's Salle Louis-Fréchette. ©Louise Leblanc

▼ A splendid view from the Observatoire de la Capitale. ©CCNQ, Pierre Joosten

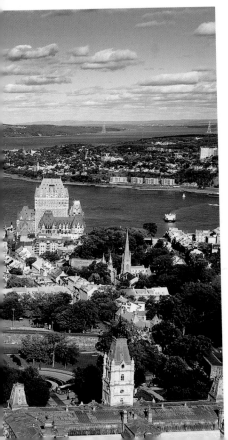

which belongs to the organisation Jardins du Québec, is open to visitors. The house is also home to the Conseil des Monuments et Sites de Québec.

Avenue Cartier is one of the most attractive shopping streets in town. The main artery in the Montcalm residential neighbourhood, it is lined with restaurants, shops and specialty food stores that attract shoppers and strollers.

Also in the area are the American-style **Maison Pollack**; the Renaissance Revival **Foyer Néo-Renaissance des Dames Protestantes**, built in 1862 by architect Michel Lecourt; and **Maison Krieghoff**, which was occupied in 1859 by the Dutch painter Cornelius Krieghoff.

The **Monastère des Dominicains** and its church are relatively recent testimonials to the persistence and historical exactitude of 20th-century Gothic Revival architecture. This sober British-style building promotes reverence and meditation.

Located at the roundabout of Avenue Wolfe-Montcalm is the **Monument to General Wolfe**, victor of the decisive Battle of the Plains of Abraham. It is said to stand on the exact spot where he fell. The 1832 monument has been the object

Grande Allée

of countless demonstrations and acts of vandalism. Toppled again in 1963, it was rebuilt, this time with an inscription in French.

At the heart of the splendid Battlefields Park, the **Musée National des Beaux-Arts du Québec** was built in 1933 and formerly known as the Musée de la Province de Québec. The museum is a work of art in itself, with its sculptured ceilings, columns topped with capitals, noble materials and graceful forms.

The exhibition space was enlarged and renovated in 1989-1991, and now includes three buildings: the neoclassical Pavillon Gérard-Morisset; the Pavillon Charles-Baillairgé, formerly the city prison; and the Grand Hall, a transparent building that links the two others and serves as the main entrance. At dusk, the museum is floodlit to show off its beautiful architecture.

A visit to this important museum allows one to become acquainted with the painting, sculpture and jewellery of Québec from the time of New France to today. The museum houses nearly 33,000 works from the 17th century to the present. One of the 12 galleries is devoted to painter Jean Paul Riopelle and features his huge (42m) mural *L'Hommage à Rosa Luxemburg*; another is devoted to artist Alfred Pellan.

The collections of religious art gathered from Québec's rural parishes are particularly interesting. Also on display are official documents, including the original surrender of Québec (1759). The museum frequently hosts temporary exhibits from the United States and Europe.

Now a living history of Québec art, the Musée National des Beaux-Arts du Québec will continue to grow thanks to a major expansion project scheduled to be completed by 2012. New gallery space will allow a larger part of its important collection to be displayed.

In July 1759, a British fleet commanded by General Wolfe arrived in front of Québec City and an attack was launched almost immediately. Almost 40,000 cannonballs crashed down on the besieged city. As the summer drew to a close, the British had to make a decision before they were surprised by French reinforcements or trapped in the December freeze. On the 13th of September, under cover of night, British troops scaled the Cap Diamant escarpment west of the fortifications. The ravines that cut into the otherwise

▸   Avenue Cartier, an attractive shopping street. ©Philippe Renault/Hemis

▸   One of the galleries of the Musée National des Beaux-Arts du Québec. ©Philippe Renault/Hemis

▸   The Musée National des Beaux-Arts du Québec. ©Les Photographes Kedl, 2004

Grande Allée

▲   The Plains of Abraham: nature in the heart of the city. ©Philippe Renault/Hemis

uniform mass of the escarpment allowed them to climb while remaining concealed. By morning, the troops had taken position in the fields of Abraham Martin, hence the name given to the park: **Plains of Abraham**. The French were surprised, as they had anticipated a direct attack on the citadel. Their troops, with the aid of a few hundred Aboriginal and (French-) Canadian fighters, threw themselves against the British. The generals of both sides were slain, and the battle drew to a close in bloody chaos. New France was lost.

Battlefields Park (Parc des Champs-de-Bataille), the site of the Battle of the Plains of Abraham, was created in 1908 to commemorate the event. The splendid 101ha park overlooking the St. Lawrence River is to Québec City what Parc du Mont-Royal is to Montréal or Central Park to New York: the city's chief nature oasis.

Previously occupied by a military training ground, the Ursuline order of nuns, and a few farms, the park was laid out between 1929 and 1939 by landscape architect Frederick Todd.

Grande Allée

This project provided work for thousands of Québécois during the Depression. Today, the plains are a large green space crisscrossed with paths used for all kinds of winter and summer activities. You will find beautiful landscaping here as well as historical and cultural sites such as the **Kiosque Edwin-Bélanger**, which presents outdoor entertainment.

Martello Towers no. 1 and no. 2 are characteristic of British defenses at the beginning of the 19th century. Tower number 1 (1808) is visible from the edge of Avenue Ontario; number 2 (1815) blends into the surrounding buildings on the corner of Avenue Laurier and Avenue Taché. Inside the first tower, an exhibition recounts some of the military strategies used in the 19th century. At Martello Tower no. 2, you can enjoy murder-mystery dinners with characters from 1814 in period dress, whom you join in unmasking the culprit in a sinister plot. A third tower stands to the north at the other end of the cape, in the Faubourg Saint-Jean-Baptiste.

Grande Allée

Faubourg Saint-Jean-Baptiste

A lively neighbourhood since its beginnings, complete with concert halls, bars, cafés, bistros and boutiques, the charming Faubourg Saint-Jean-Baptiste, full of life 24 hours a day, is perched on a hillside between the Haute-Ville and Basse-Ville. It hosts a varied crowd of busy residents and carefree passers-by. The abundance of pitched and mansard roofs is reminiscent of parts of the old city, but the orthogonal layout of the streets is quintessentially North American. Despite a terrible fire in 1845, this former suburb retains several examples of wooden construction, which was forbidden inside the city's walls.

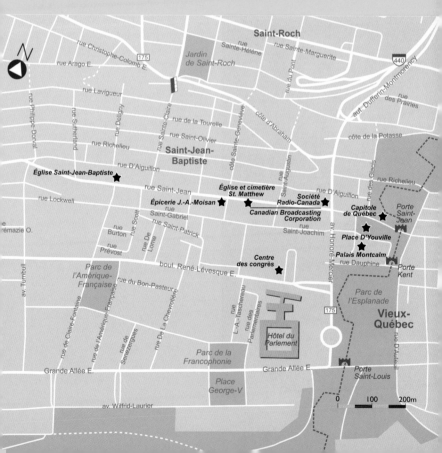

Place D'Youville, commonly called "carré D'Youville" (D'Youville square) by Québec residents, is a major public space at the entrance of the old town. Formerly an important market square, today it is a bustling crossroads and cultural forum. Redevelopment has given the square a large promenade area with trees and benches; a large kiosk serves as a meeting spot. The counterscarp wall, part of the fortifications that were removed in the 19th century, has been highlighted by the use of black granite blocks. In October, part of the square is covered in ice, much to the delight of skaters.

▼   The Capitole de Québec. ©Pierre Phaneuf

▼   Place D'Youville by night. ©Jonathan Habel

At the western end of the Place D'Youville stands *Les Muses*, a majestic bronze sculpture by Alfred Laliberté (1878-1953). The six muses represent music, oratory, poetry, architecture, sculpture and painting.

At the beginning of the 20th century, Québec City was in dire need of a new auditorium, its Académie de Musique having burnt to the ground in March 1900. With the help of private enterprise, the mayor undertook the search for a new location. The Canadian government, owner of the fortifications, offered to provide a strip of land along the walls of the city. Although narrow, the lot grew wider toward the back, permitting the construction of a suitable hall, the **Capitole de Québec**. W. S. Painter, the ingenious Detroit architect who was already at work on the expansion of the Château Frontenac, devised a plan for a curved facade, giving the building a monumental air despite the limited size of the lot. Inaugurated in 1903 as the Auditorium de Québec, the building is one of the most impressive *beaux-arts* creations in the country.

In 1927, the famous American cinema architect Thomas W. Lamb converted the auditorium into a sumptuous 1,700-seat cinema. Renamed the Théâtre du Capitole, the auditorium nevertheless served as a venue for live shows until the construction of the Grand Théâtre in 1971. Abandoned for a few years, the Capitole was entirely refurbished in 1992 by architect Denis Saint-Louis. The building now houses a dinner-theatre in its hall, a luxury hotel and a restaurant within the curved facade. The Capitole has recently acquired the adjoining cinema, with its imposing round marquee; it has been converted into a nightclub.

▲   The skating rink on Place D'Youville. ©Jonathan Houle

The Montcalm Market was levelled in 1932 to build the **Palais Montcalm**. Formerly the venue of choice for political rallies and demonstrations of all kinds, the auditorium has a spare architecture which draws on both the neoclassical and Art Deco schools. The Palais was recently renovated and now welcomes music lovers to a splendid concert hall, Salle Raoul-Jobin. One of its most important occupants is the world-renowned Violons du Roy chamber orchestra. The Palais' rear facade has been enhanced by Québec artist Florent Cousineau's work *Le Fil Rouge*. Visible from Rue Dauphine, the work consists of three stone bas-reliefs linked by a thread of light.

The **Chapelle du Couvent des Sœurs de la Charité** (1856) is visible on leaving Place d'Youville. Its delicate Gothic Revival facade is dwarfed by two huge towers.

The red brick building at no. 888 Rue Saint-Jean houses the Québec City radio and television studios of the **Canadian Broadcasting Corporation** (Radio-Canada). Speakers on the sidewalk play the current radio broadcast.

Avenue Honoré-Mercier is home to Paul Béliveau's work *Les Vents Déferlants*. The allegorical piece consists of two groups of three masts on either side of Rue Saint-Jean, representing Jacques Cartier's ships arriving at the Iroquois village of Stadaconé in 1535.

Higher up on Avenue Honoré-Mercier, at the corner of Rue Saint-Joachim, is a large network of buildings that includes the Centre des Congrès (convention centre), the Place Québec shopping centre and the Hilton Québec and Delta Québec hotels.

Faubourg Saint-Jean-Baptiste

▲ The magnificent Salle Raoul-Jobin, in Palais Montcalm. ©Philippe Renault/Hemis

Faubourg Saint-Jean-Baptiste

The **Centre des Congrès de Québec** was inaugurated in 1996 and is situated north of the Hôtel du Parlement. This large modern building features glass walls that let the daylight stream in. It includes an exhibition hall, several conference rooms and even a ballroom, and is connected to the Place Québec shopping centre and the Hilton Québec and Delta Québec hotels. Its creation has revived this pre-viously dreary part of Boulevard René-Lévesque. Between the Hilton Québec hotel and the Centre des Congrès is the **Promenade Desjardins**, which recalls the life and work of Alphonse Desjardins, the founder of the Caisses Populaires Des-jardins credit union. At the end of the promenade is a great view of the city and the faraway mountains. At the entrance

to the Centre des Congrès is the lively sculpture *Le Quatuor d'Airain*, the work of Lucienne Payan-Cornet.

There has been a cemetery on the site of **St. Matthew's Church and Cemetery** since 1771, when Protestants, whether French Huguenot, English Anglican or Scottish Presbyterian, banded together to found a Protestant graveyard. Several 19th-century tombstones are still standing. The gravestones were carefully restored recently, and the cemetery is now a public garden.

Located in the cemetery along Rue Saint-Jean is a lovely Anglican church. Its Gothic Revival architecture was influenced by the Ecclesiologists, an influential school of Anglican thought that sought to

Faubourg Saint-Jean-Baptiste

re-establish ties with the traditions of the Middle Ages. In its design, and even in its materials, it looks more like an ancient village church than a Victorian church with a Gothic decor. The nave was first erected in 1848; then, in 1870, William Tutin Thomas, the Montréal architect who designed Shaughnessy House (now part of Montréal's Canadian Centre of Architecture), drafted an enlargement, giving the church its present bell tower and interior. Québec's Anglican community dwindled in the 20th century, leading to the abandonment of the church. In 1980,

◄ The modern Centre des Congrès de Québec. ©sccq

it was cleverly converted into a branch of the municipal library. Several of the adornments crafted by British artists have been retained: Percy Bacon's handsome oak choir enclosure, Felix Morgan's alabaster pulpit, and Clutterbuck's beautiful stained glass. The sober vault with its exposed beams is also noteworthy.

Épicerie J.-A.-Moisan was founded in 1871 and claims to be the "oldest grocery store in North America." It does in fact look like a general store from yesteryear, with its wooden floor and shelves, old advertisements and tin cans.

The **Église Saint-Jean-Baptiste** stands out as Joseph Ferdinand Peachy's masterpiece. A disciple of French eclecticism, Peachy was a wholehearted admirer of the Église de la Trinité in Paris. The resemblance here is striking, as much in the portico as in the interior. Completed in 1885, the building caused the bankruptcy of its architect, who was, unfortunately for him, held responsible for cracks that appeared in the facade during construction. In front of the church is an attractive little square.

For a beautiful view of the city, take the Rue Claire-Fontaine stairs up to the corner of Rue Lockwell, on the right. The climb is steep but the view is worth the effort, especially in the evening when the lights of the Basse-Ville dance at your feet behind the imposing church. When strolling through this neighbourhood's attractive streets, you will have many opportunities to catch a glimpse of this great view. For example, you can go down Rue Sainte-Claire to the stairs or the Faubourg elevator leading to the Saint-Roch neighbourhood, which you will be able to see with the Laurentian mountains in the background.

◀ Épicerie J.-A. Moisan, founded in 1871.
©Patrick Donovan

Faubourg Saint-Jean-Baptiste

Saint-Roch and Saint-Sauveur

The Saint-Roch neighbourhood, bounded by Cap Diamant to the south, Boulevard Langelier to the west, the Rivière Saint-Charles to the north, and the Autoroute Dufferin-Montmorency to the east, formerly suffered from a poor reputation that contributed to a cycle of decay. Nowadays, however, it enjoys a new vitality and is more popular than ever before. The "Nouvo" Saint-Roch, younger and more energetic, is a lively and interesting area to visit on foot.

Compared to frenetic neighbouring Saint-Roch, the charming Saint-Sauveur neighbourhood is an oasis of calm. But Saint-Sauveur is also considered the multicultural face of Québec City: its central artery, Rue Saint-Vallier, is lined with little restaurants and boutiques run by new Quebecers from Mexico, the Caribbean, Africa and Asia. With its narrow streets and "dollhouse" buildings, it draws crowds to enjoy world cuisine at reasonable prices in a relaxing atmosphere.

Saint-Roch

SAINT-ROCH

Originally settled by potters and tanners at the end of the French regime, Saint-Roch slowly developed along Rue De Saint-Vallier. Then, when the Napoleonic blockade forced Great Britain to rely on its colonies for its wood supply, huge shipyards were created on the banks of Rivière Saint-Charles. This attracted a large working-class population to Saint-Roch. A cholera epidemic in 1832 rav-aged the area and almost a quarter of its inhabitants died. Floods then devastated it in both 1845 and 1866. The neighbour-hood saw its largest industry disappear in just a few years when France and Britain returned to normal relations and ships began using metal hulls (1860-1870).

This marked the beginning of a com-plete transformation that would make Saint-Roch one of the main industrial quarters in French Canada. A number of

The Rivière Saint-Charles, known to the Hurons as Kabir Kouba. ©Patrick Donovan

◄ A view of Jardin de Saint-Roch from the Haute-Ville. ©Société du 400ᵉ anniversaire de Québec

days. However, in the early 20th century, the well-to-do who still lived here left Saint-Roch to settle in the Haute-Ville, mainly on Grande Allée. Then, during the 1960s, commercial activity experienced increasing competition from the suburbs and gradually declined; as a result, department stores and factories were forced to shut down and the neglected neighbourhood was all but forgotten for the next few decades.

In the mid-1990s, construction and revitalization projects began at a rather slow pace, then took off at an unprecedented speed, completely transforming Saint-Roch. In 1992, the city launched an action plan intended to give this former commercial centre a little of its old vitality.

This began with the creation of a lovely park, the Jardin de Saint-Roch, an ideal place for a stroll, which has caused residents and developers to regain an interest in the district. Several businesses (especially in the multimedia fields), schools such as the École des Arts Visuels de l'Université Laval and the École Nationale

factories were created to produce goods for popular consumption (tobacco, shoes, clothing, furniture), in keeping with the tradition of 18th-century potters and tanners. Next to them, department stores such as Paquet, Pollack and the Syndicat de Québec all established themselves on Boulevard Charest, completing the district's commercial activities. Like the workers, factory and shop owners were French Canadians, a phenomenon that was rarely seen in Canada in those

Saint-Roch

d'Administration Publique (ÉNAP), and theatres and other cultural sites are now established in Saint-Roch.

Rue De Saint-Vallier (west of Boulevard Langelier, it is called Rue Saint-Vallier, without the preposition), between Côte du Palais and Côte d'Abraham, has been disfigured in many places, particularly by the construction of the Dufferin-Montmorency Expressway ramps in 1970. It nevertheless shows evidence of a very interesting past.

At number 870, you can see the ruins of the **Maison Blanche**, the secondary residence of Charles-Aubert de la Chesnaye, a wealthy merchant. The house was built in 1679 by architect Claude Baillif. In 1845, it was severely damaged by a fire

▼ One of the works presented at Méduse, a multimedia art complex. ©*Philippe Renault/Hemis*

▼ Jardin de Saint-Roch, a delightful green oasis. ©*Patrick Donovan*

and only half of it was salvaged. Today, only the arches and a few sections of wall remain from the original house.

A little further along are two cast iron and wood staircases designed by Charles Baillairgé. One was constructed in 1883 and the other in 1889. Upon completion they connected the geographically and socially separate worlds of the city below and the city above. At number 715, a group of well-preserved buildings belongs to the Lépine-Cloutier Funeral Home, which has been in operation since 1845.

Wedged between Rue De Saint-Vallier and Côte d'Abraham, **Méduse** houses various artists' associations that support and promote Québec culture. Encompassing restored houses and modern buildings that integrate the city's architecture, the multi-use complex is perched on the side of Cap Diamant, linking the Haute-Ville and Basse-Ville. Associations in various fields such as photography, printmaking and video have their offices here, as well as studios and galleries. Radio Basse-Ville, a community radio station, and the Abraham-Martin restaurant are also located on the premises. Running along the east side is a stairway which links Côte d'Abraham to Rue De Saint-Vallier.

At the corner of Côte d'Abraham and Rue de la Couronne, you will find a rock garden with a waterfall known as the **Jardin de Saint-Roch**. The creation of this park was considered the first step in the rejuvenation of this neighbourhood.

Beside the Ascenseur du Faubourg, to enhance the neighbouring apartment block's parking lot, artist Florent Cousineau created *La Falaise Apprivoisée*, an imposing structure of steel strips over the cliff face, crowned by a rooftop garden that twinkles with firefly-like lights at night.

▲ La Fabrique, in the former Dominion Corset factory. ©Philippe Renault/Hemis

The section of Rue De Saint-Vallier between Rue Dorchester and Boulevard Langelier is livelier now that a charming inn as well as bistros, bars, restaurants, shops and hair salons have sprung up. At the corner of Rue Victor-Révillon, another public work of art by Florent Cousineau, *La Chute de Mots*, occupies the corner of a building. An array of words is supported by a cascade of illuminated metal bands.

La Fabrique is located in the former Dominion Corset factory which, as its name indicates, was a manufacturer of corsets and brassieres. President Georges Amyot built this enormous factory between 1897 and 1911, creating jobs for the abundant workforce of young unmarried women. Because Amyot believed a married woman's place was in the home and not the factory, marriage meant immediate dismissal. The former

Saint-Roch

Dominion Corset factory was restored and renamed "La Fabrique" in 1993. It now houses an interpretation centre recounting Québec City's rich industrial past, the **Service du Développement Économique**, as well as the **École des Arts Visuels de l'Université Laval**. Take a look at the facade's complex brickwork, the clocktower and the water tower, elements that are reminiscent of American factory architecture of the end of the 19th century.

Boulevard Charest was created in 1928 to relieve this neighbourhood's congested narrow streets, since the roads built between 1790 and 1840 were no longer able to handle commercial and industrial traffic. There are a few prominent buildings on Boulevard Charest which once housed Québec City's department stores. Today they are all closed. At number 740 is the former Pollack store, dating from 1950. The back of the old Paquet store can still be found at the corner of Rue du Parvis, and at the corner of Rue de la Couronne, you can see the Syndicat de Québec, rebuilt in 1949 and shut down in 1981. The building was renovated and transformed into an office building in 2002.

Église Notre-Dame-de-Jacques-Cartier was originally the Saint-Roch Congregationalists' chapel. It was built in 1853 and expanded in 1875. In 1901, it brought together an entire parish. Its interior was richly decorated by Raphaël Giroux and includes lateral rood screens adorned with gold columns. At the back of the church is the stately embossed-stone presbytery constructed in 1902, but most noteworthy is its tilted steeple!

If you stroll around a bit, you'll see some of the **Saint-Roch workers' houses**, which are unique to Québec City's Basse-Ville. Compact and erected at the edge of the sidewalk, they are made of brownish brick or, occasionally, wood. They have sloping or mansard roofs and shuttered French windows. The architecture could be described as a kind of hybrid between North American working-class and French industrial-town architecture.

▼ The rich interior of Église Notre-Dame-de-Jacques-Cartier. ©*Conseil du patrimoine religieux du Québec, 2003*

▲ The Impérial de Québec theatre.
   ©Impérial de Québec

▲ On Rue Saint-Joseph, a former post office is
   now home to a restaurant. ©Patrick Donovan

At the beginning of the 19th century, as Saint-Roch was rapidly developing, many wooden houses spring up, which were inspired by the French Regime's country houses. But the great fire of 1845 reduced the neighbourhood to ashes and changed the rules of the game. After the fire, brick or stone construction became mandatory and wood ornamentation was discouraged. These rules were softened at the end of the 19th century and several houses were then decorated with Victorian wood trim. But the face of Saint-Roch did not change significantly and has kept its quaint, old-time image to this day.

The **Impérial de Québec** theatre wore many masks over the years before its 2003 reopening. Built in 1917 and destroyed by fire in 1933, it reopened the same year and became the Cinéma de Paris. It was renamed the Midi-Minuit in 1971, then Les Folies de Paris in 1996. Whatever the name, the Impérial's story-book auditorium and La Casbah bistro have won the hearts of the neighbourhood just as the Théâtre du Capitole did in the Faubourg Saint-Jean-Baptiste.

In 1831, the creation of a marketplace was planned at the corner of Rue Saint-Joseph and Rue de la Couronne, but it was only in 1857 that two of its halls were actually built. One of them burned down in 1911, and the other was demolished around 1930 to create **Place Jacques-Cartier**. The statue of the famous explorer, which can be seen at the centre of the square, was given by the city of Saint-Malo, France, Cartier's birthplace, in 1924.

At the far end, **Bibliothèque Gabrielle-Roy**, built in 1982-1983, was named for one of French Canada's most famous writers, who lived in Québec City for many years. Her most famous novel, *The Tin Flute* (*Bonheur d'occasion*), detailed the misery of a working-class Montréal neighbourhood in the 1930s. The municipal library also offers special exhibition spaces to promote the work of contemporary artists.

The eastern section of **Rue Saint-Joseph** was once covered by a glass roof and was part of the Mail Centre-Ville. Since the year 2000, the roof has been removed from mall to transform it into a small-town shopping street, where cafés and shops make strolling a charming experience. You'll notice that this wind of revival has also affected the block that stretches west of the library, where a wide array of theatres, bookstores, inns and restaurants await you.

Saint-Roch

Surprisingly, none of the working-class neighbourhoods have kept their old churches. Fire and the rapidly-increasing population have meant that larger and more modern buildings have replaced the old churches. The first **Église Saint-Roch** was erected around 1811 and was replaced by two other buildings before the present church was built between 1916 and 1923. It is an immense neo-Romanesque structure with two steeples and a rather austere interior; however, it features interesting stained-glass windows made by the Montréal firm Hobbs (around 1920). Stuck behind the Mail Centre-Ville, Église Saint-Roch was almost forgotten in recent years. But the revitalization of Rue Saint-Joseph gave the church and its square a prime spot in the neighbourhood. Its facade is inspired by that of Notre-Dame Cathedral in Paris.

Rue du Pont was named as such when the first Pont Dorchester was inaugurated in 1789 at the north end of the street. The bridge crosses Rivière Saint-Charles and links Limoilou and the northern sector of Québec City, and has been rebuilt many times. You can still find remnants of the French Regime settlement east of Rue du Pont. This area, which reaches as far as the columns of the Dufferin-Montmorency Expressway, is where the Récollet Fathers' Saint-Roch Hermitage was situated, giving its name to the area.

In 1692, after giving up their Saint-Sauveur monastery to Monseigneur de Saint-Vallier so that it could be turned into a hospital, the Récollets settled in the east where they built a hermitage (retreat) for their priests. The hermitage consisted of a large house with an adjoining chapel; both have since disappeared. Later, a small village was created and businesses were started, populating the area.

SAINT-SAUVEUR

The history of Saint-Sauveur began in 1615 when the Récollets came to the banks of Rivière Saint-Charles. These reformed Franciscans had great plans for their land. They anticipated bringing 300 families from France who would settle in a town called "Ludovica." In 1621, they built the first stone church in New France. Unfortunately, when the Kirke brothers captured Québec City in 1629, the project was brought to a halt and, despite the return to French rule in 1632, the Récollets' colonization project never went any further. Only their monastery was rebuilt before being bought by the Bishop of Québec City to create the Hôpital Général (1693).

It was only after the great fire destroyed the neighbouring quarter of Saint-Roch (1845) that Saint-Sauveur became urbanized. In great confusion, hundreds of small wooden houses were built on meagre and often unsanitary plots of land. In 1866 and again in 1889, major fires ravaged much of the neighbourhood, which nevertheless continued to attract a number of general workers.

Québec writer Roger Lemelin (1919-1994) has made the neighbourhood of his childhood and romances well known through his work. His novels *Au pied de la pente douce* (1944) and *Les Plouffe* (1948) have been made into television series and films. He describes the harsh day-to-day life of the people of Saint-Sauveur while showing both their shortcomings and their kind-heartedness. At the time, this working-class quarter of the Basse-Ville located west of Saint-Roch was Québec City's poorest neighbourhood and had the city's highest unemployment rate.

▶ The majestic facade of Église Saint-Roch.
©Philippe Renault/Hemis

SAUVONS L'ÉGLISE SAINT-ROCH

The small houses with mansard roofs on **Rue Victoria** and the surrounding streets give the neighbourhood a friendly village atmosphere. These dwellings were constructed on the tiniest possible plots of land by owners who wanted to fit a maximum number of families into a minimum of space. At the beginning of the 20th century, some houses were expanded with extra storeys, along with balconies and richly ornamented bay windows.

Église Saint-Sauveur stands at the north end of Rue Victoria. It was erected in 1867, re-using the original burnt walls of the first church built in 1851. Architect Joseph-Ferdinand Peachy designed a neo-Romanesque facade with a spire to give it a Baroque look. Abundantly decorated at the end of the 19th century, the interior has a slender nave and is surrounded by high lateral galleries. Note the windows by Beaulieu and Rochon (1897).

A stroll down **Rue Saint-Vallier** (east of Boulevard Langelier, it is called Rue De Saint-Vallier, with the preposition) leads you into the heart of the lively Saint-Sauveur neighbourhood, with its snack bars, Asian restaurants, curiosity shops and artists' studios. There are also a number of old aristocratic houses with balconies and turrets.

Parc Victoria was created in 1897 to provide the neighbourhoods of Saint-Roch and Saint-Sauveur with some green space, an element that had been missing until then. Pathways and rustic log structures were built and became very popular among city dwellers. But the park lost some of its appeal when the bend in Rivière Saint-Charles was filled in, since the river had almost completely encircled the park at that time.

The Récollets built the first stone church in New France in 1621 on the site of the **Hôpital Général**. Their plan was to bring 300 families from France and settle on the banks of Rivière Saint-Charles in a village

▲   The Moulin de l'Hôpital-Général.
©Hélène Huard

called "Ludovica." Although this project never came to fruition, the institution slowly grew and took root. The present chapel was built in 1673, and in 1682 the Récollets added an arched cloister to their monastery. A few parts remain and have been integrated into the subsequent additions.

In 1693, Monseigneur Jean-Baptiste de la Croix de Chevrières de Saint-Vallier, the second Bishop of Québec City, bought the monastery from the Récollets to establish a hospital. The Augustine Hospitaller Order of the Hôtel-Dieu took charge of the institution, which looked after destitute, disabled and elderly people. Today the Hôpital Général is a modern institution for long-term-care patients. However, a great deal of its past has been preserved—more, in fact, than any other institution of its kind in Québec City. There are many elements from the 17th and 18th centuries, such as the Récollets' cells, woodwork, dispensary cupboards and painted panelling. Fortunately, the hospital was never damaged by fire and only slightly by the bombardments of the conquest, a rarity in Québec City.

It is not possible to visit these vestiges, but you can take a tour of the **Musée du Monastère des Augustines** and the small Église Notre-Dame-des-Anges. This church was redecorated in 1770 by

Saint-Sauveur

▲ The Mémorial à la Guerre de Sept Ans. ©CCNQ, Paul Dionne

Pierre Émond and houses the preciously guarded tabernacle created in 1722 by François-Noël Levasseur. There are some beautiful paintings, such as *L'Assomption de la Vierge* by Frère Luc, painted here during the artist's visit to Canada in 1670, and several paintings by Joseph Légaré bought in 1824.

You can also visit the **Military Cemetery**, where many of the soldiers who died during the Battle of the Plains of Abraham are buried. There is also a mausoleum where the remains of the Marquis de Montcalm now rest, and nearby is the **Mémorial à la Guerre de Sept Ans**, along with a sculpture by Pascale Archambault named *Traversée sans retour*. This memorial honours the memory of the 1,058 soldiers who died between 1755 and 1760 and are buried here. In addition to French and British soldiers, French Canadians and Aboriginals who died trying to defend their land are also interred here.

The **École Technique** or École des Métiers, is a good example of Québec City's Beaux-Arts architecture. This is a major architectural work by René Pamphile Lemay that was built between 1909 and 1911. The long red-brick and stone building had a 22m-high central tower that was unfortunately demolished around 1955.

The **Moulin de l'Hôpital-Général** stands in the middle of a small park at the corner of Avenue Langelier and Rue Saint-François. This old windmill is the only one of about 20 to have survived the harshness of Québec's climate. Its stone tower was erected on earlier foundations in 1730 for the nuns and patients of the Hôpital Général. It milled grain until 1862, when a fire destroyed it completely. The mill was then integrated into an industrial building and was concealed so that it disappeared from view. Only in 1976 was the tower, or what remained of it, uncovered and given a new roof.

Saint-Sauveur

Limoilou

As the winter of 1535 approached, Jacques Cartier, who was on his second exploration trip to Canada, had to find a good anchorage for his fleet before it was trapped by ice in the middle of the St. Lawrence River. He discovered a well-protected harbour in the bend of Rivière Saint-Charles and had a small log fort built. Towering above it, a wooden cross with the coat of arms of François I was erected. Thus, Limoilou became the first French settlement in Canada. However, after Jacques Cartier left, the fort disappeared. Today, the Cartier-Brébeuf National Historic Site marks the area.

In 1625, the territory was granted to the Jesuits. They created the Seigneurie de Notre-Dame-des-Anges here and had colonists settle and cultivate the land. It was only in the middle of the 19th century that Limoilou started to urbanize, taking advantage of the prosperity of Saint-Roch's shipyards on the other side of Rivière Saint-Charles.

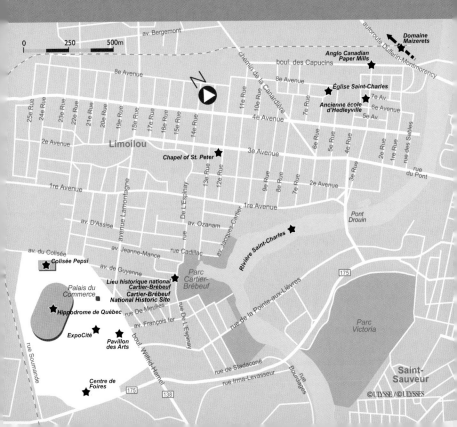

Large estates began to appear, each with fields, warehouses, a working-class village and, on the outskirts, the owner's residence surrounded by a landscaped garden. However, little of this period now remains. It was only at the beginning of the 20th century that the present neighbourhood took shape and acquired its name. Limoilou refers to the Manoir de Limoilou near Saint-Malo, France, where Cartier retired after his numerous trips to New France.

▲ Bucolic Rivière Saint-Charles. ©Gilbert Bochenek

Aboriginal Peoples called the river *Kabir Kouba*, meaning "river with many bends," and in 1535, Cartier renamed it "Rivière Sainte-Croix." The Récollets who settled on the southern banks in 1615 gave the river its present name, **Rivière Saint-Charles**, in honour of Pontoise priest Charles de Boves, who had financed their establishment in New France. The river crosses the rich alluvial plain at the foot of Cap Diamant, going through the centre of the Basse-Ville and isolating Limoilou from other working-class neighbourhoods. The river is made up of numerous meanders which end in what used to be a swampy estuary, but is now the Port de Québec and Bassin Louise.

During the Conquest of 1763, the Jesuits lost their right to teach in Canada. The last of them died in Québec City at the end of the 18th century, and the Notre-Dame-des-Anges seigneury was taken over by the King of Great Britain, who redistributed the land. Around 1845, William Hedley Anderson created Hedleyville on his portion of land. It was the first village in what is now Limoilou to specialize in naval construction and the wood trade. Only a few buildings remain from the village, which was located between 1re and 3e Rues and between 4e and 7e Avenues. At 699 3e Rue is the former **École d'Hedleyville**, a school constructed in 1863 to provide workers' children with a basic education. The school's

architecture is not much different from the neighbourhood's wooden dwellings and was converted to housing quite a while ago.

Go to the end of 3e Rue at the corner of Boulevard des Capucins, where you can admire, between the pillars of the Dufferin-Montmorency Highway, the view of the former **Anglo Canadian Paper Mills**. This gigantic red-brick industrial complex looks like an impregnable stronghold and was erected in 1928 on land reclaimed from the Rivière Saint-Charles estuary.

Beautiful **Église Saint-Charles-de-Limoilou** stands at the corner of 5e Rue, offering a pleasant view. The church and conventional buildings surrounding it were all erected on a strip of land that once belonged to Québec City's Hôtel-Dieu. Built with a typical neo-Romanesque facade (1917-1920), the nave of the Limoilou parish church has a double row of medieval-looking arches designed by architect Joseph-Pierre Ouellet. Its interior is representative of Québec City's parish churches, which are generally narrower and taller than most churches in other regions of Québec. In this manner, the influence of the Notre-Dame de Québec Cathedral, a tall, narrow Baroque work from the mid-18th century, seems to have been felt locally right up until the Second World War.

Limoilou

▲ The monument to Jacques Cartier and Chief Donnacona, at the Cartier-Brébeuf National Historic Site. ©Patrick Donovan

Along 5e Rue are located several of Limoilou's civic buildings, such as the beautiful Beaux-Arts fire station constructed in 1910 by the City of Québec. The city had annexed the formerly autonomous municipality of Limoilou the previous year, making it part of Québec City.

On **Domaine Maizerets** is the Maizerets house, one of the former summer residences of the Séminaire de Québec. The first house was built in 1697 and has been expanded three times since. It was first known as the Domaine de la Canardière because of the innumerable ducks (*canards*) that nested on the nearby sandbars. The house was then given the name "Domaine de Maizerets" in homage to Louis Ango de Maizerets, the superior of the Québec City seminary at the time. The house, its farm and its park are a rare group of 18th-century rural developments in the Québec City region that are still intact. Its gardens, part of the Association des Jardins du Québec, are a pleasant spot to relax.

The **Chapel of St. Peter** bears witness to the Anglo-Saxon Anglican presence in Limoilou during the 1920s and 1930s. Most worshippers were managerial staff or owners of the nearby factories, and the Anglican bishop had this chapel built especially for them. However, their numbers were never sufficient enough to justify transforming the chapel into a large church.

The streets around the chapel offer good examples of the architecture of Limoilou houses; their resemblance to those in Montréal is not accidental. In fact, Limoilou saw itself as a "modern" town—later a neighbourhood—modelling itself after other North American towns at the beginning of the 20th century. Developers from Montréal as well as the United States sold lots requiring Montréal-style constructions such as flat roofs, multi-level balconies, exterior metal staircases, parapets, alleyways and sheds. Even the shaded streets and avenues were given numbers instead of names, in all-American fashion.

Limoilou

Cartier-Brébeuf National Historic Site is located on the spot where Jacques Cartier and his crew spent the winter of 1535-1536. The difficult conditions of this forced winter stay, which resulted in the death of 25 sailors, are explained at the reception and interpretation centre. A scale model of Cartier's fort is also displayed there. One must remember that Cartier's plan was not to establish a colony on Canadian soil but rather to make more lucrative discoveries, such as a passage to China or minerals as precious as the gold of the Spanish colonies.

This historic site is a pleasant green space spread out around an inlet of Rivière Saint-Charles. Bike paths cross it, leading to the Vieux-Port and Montmorency Falls. This was once the mouth of Rivière Lairet, but today it has been filled in. You can see a model of an Iroquois Long House showing Aboriginal living arrangements in the St. Lawrence River Valley at the time of the first explorers, when Jacques Cartier arrived at the village of Stadaconé near the site of present-day Québec City. But Cartier is not the only person whose memory is honoured at this historic site. Saint Jean de Brébeuf (1593-1649), a Jesuit missionary martyred by the Iroquois, arrived here in 1625 to establish the Notre-Dame-des-Anges seigneury. A monument commemorating both men was inaugurated in 1889. The Cartier-Brébeuf National Historic Site has a pleasant walkway that runs along the meandering Rivière Saint-Charles to the south.

The **Colisée Pepsi**, formerly and commonly still called the Colisée de Québec, is an indoor arena where the Québec Nordiques, the city's beloved former major-league hockey team, used to play. The Colisée was built in 1950 by an architect of Swiss origin, Robert Blatter, who is also responsible for several attractive international-style houses in Sillery. Renovated and modernized in 1979, the arena is now the permanent home of the Les Remparts hockey team and hosts international-scale concerts and shows.

The Colisée was built on the site of **ExpoCité**, which also hosts the **Hippodrome de Québec**, built in 1916 and formerly called Palais Central, as well as the

▼ Québec City's sprawling Centre de Foires. ©ExpoCité

Pavillon des Arts, built in 1913. These two Beaux-Arts buildings have hosted the annual Exposition provinciale since 1892, and suggest the pavilions of the Chicago World's Fair of 1893. ExpoCité also hosts the vast **Centre de Foires** (1997), designed specially to host the numerous trade shows and fairs that attract the residents of the capital and its surroundings.

▼ Cartier-Brébeuf National Historic Site in autumn. ©Eric Beaulieu

Sillery and Sainte-Foy

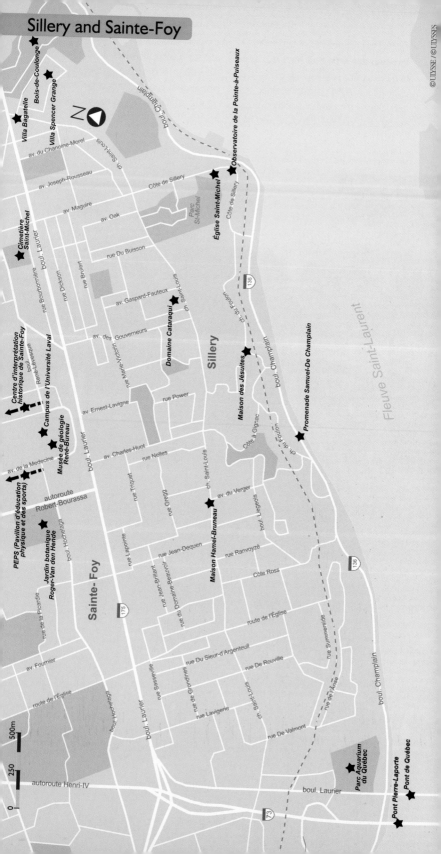

Villa Bagatelle

Bois-de-Coulonge

Villa Spencer Grange

av. du Chanoine-Morel

av. Joseph-Rousseau

ch. Saint-Louis

boul. Chauplain

Côte de Sillery

av. Maguire

av. Oak

Parc St-Michel

Église Saint-Michel

Observatoire de la Pointe-à-Puiseaux

Côte de Sillery

Côte de Puiseaux

Cimetière Saint-Michel

rue Du Buisson

136

boul. Laurier

rue Bourbonnière

rue Dickson

rue Brûlart

av. Gaspard-Fauteux

ch. Saint-Louis

Domaine Cataraqui

av. des Gouverneurs

Sillery

Maison des Jésuites

ch. du Foulon

Centre d'interprétation historique de Sainte-Foy

boul. René-Lévesque

Campus de l'Université Laval

av. Marie-Victorin

av. Ernest-Lavigne

rue Power

boul. Champlain

Promenade Samuel-De Champlain

Musée de géologie René-Bureau

av. Charles-Huot

rue Nelles

boul. Laurier

Côte à Gignac

ch. du Foulon

Fleuve Saint-Laurent

av. de la Médecine

rue Triquet

rue Gregg

ch. Saint-Louis

PEPS (Pavillon d'éducation physique et des sports)

autoroute Robert-Bourassa

av. du Verger

Maison Hamel-Bruneau

boul. Lisgeois

Jardin botanique Roger-Van den Hende

boul. Hochelaga

rue Lapointe

rue Jean-Dequen

rue Ranvoyzé

rue de la Picardie

Sainte-Foy

175

rue Jean-Brillant

rue du Domaine-Beauvoir

Côte Ross

route de l'Église

rue Summerside

136

av. Fournier

rue Sasseville

rue de Grondines

rue Du Sieur-d'Argenteuil

rue De Rouville

route de l'Église

boul. Hochelaga

boul. Laurier

rue Lavigerie

ch. Saint-Louis

rue De Valmont

rue De l'Anse

boul. Champlain

500m

250

autoroute Henri-IV

Parc Aquarium du Québec

Pont Pierre-Laporte

Pont de Québec

boul. Laurier

0

73

Sillery and Sainte-Foy

The well-to-do Québec City borough of Sillery retains many traces of its colourful past and is influenced by the sector's dramatic topography.

In 1637, the Jesuits built a mission in Sillery, on the shores of the river, with the idea of converting the Algonquins and Montagnais (Innus) who came to fish in the coves upriver from Québec City. They named the fortified community in honour of the mission's benefactor, Noël Brûlart de Sillery, an aristocrat who had been converted by St. Vincent de Paul.

By the following century, Sillery was already sought after for its beauty. The Jesuits converted their mission into a country house, and Sillery's first villa was built in 1732. Following the British Conquest, Sillery became the favoured town of administrators, military officers and British merchants, all of whom built luxurious villas on the cliff in architectural styles that were fashionable in England at the time. The splendour of these homes and their vast English gardens were in stark contrast to the simple workers' houses that were clustered at the base of the cliff. The occupants of these houses worked in the shipyards, where a fortune was being made building ships out of wood from the Outaouais region to supply the British navy during Napoleon's blockade, which began in 1806. The shipyards, set up in Sillery's sheltered coves, had all disappeared before Boulevard Champlain, now running along the river's edge, was built around 1960.

In the last few decades, Sainte-Foy has come to host some of the largest shopping malls in the province, which together constitute the second biggest tourist draw in the region after Vieux-Québec. The borough is also home to Université Laval, as well as several recreational areas that delight residents and visitors alike with their exceptional beauty all year round.

SILLERY

The **Bois-de-Coulonge** borders Chemin Saint-Louis to the east. This English park once surrounded the residence of the lieutenant-governor of Québec. The stately home was destroyed in a fire in 1966, though some of its buildings survived, notably the guard's house and the stables. The Saint-Denys stream flows through the eastern end of the grounds at the bottom of a ravine, and marks the spot where British troops gained access to the Plains of Abraham, where an historic battle decided the future of New France. Today Bois-de-Coulonge, a member of the Jardins du Québec, features magnificent gardens and an attractive arboretum.

Villa Bagatelle was once home to an attaché of the British governor, who lived on the neighbouring property of Bois-de-Coulonge. Built in 1848, the villa is a good example of 19th-century Gothic Revival residential architecture, as interpreted by American Alexander J. Davis. The house and its Victorian garden were impeccably restored in 1984 and are now open to the public. There is an interesting information centre providing background information on the villas and large estates of Sillery.

From Avenue James-LeMoine, which runs along the south side of Bagatelle, you can see the **Spencer Grange Villa**, built in 1849 for Henry Atkinson. During

▼ The marvellous Pont de Québec. ©istockphoto.com/Tony Tremblay

the Second World War, it was occupied by Zita de Bourbon-Parma, the deposed Empress of Austria.

Cimetière Saint-Michel-de-Sillery, Sillery's Catholic cemetery, is where René Lévesque (1922-1987), founder of the Parti Québecois and premier of Québec from 1976 to 1985, and his wife Corinne Côté-Lévesque (1943-2005) are buried.

Église Saint-Michel was erected in 1852 by architect George Browne. Inside are five paintings from the famous Desjardins collection. These works originally hung in Parisian churches until they were sold in 1792 following the French Revolution and brought to Québec by Abbé Desjardins.

From the **Observatoire de la Pointe-à-Puiseaux**, opposite the church square, you can see a vast panorama of the St. Lawrence River and its south shore. On the right are the bridges that link the north and south shores. The first, to the east, is the **Pont de Québec**, a cantilever bridge that was deemed an engineering marvel when it was first built. However, its construction was marked by two tragic collapses. The other bridge with great white arches is named **Pont Pierre-Laporte** in memory of the provincial government minister who was abducted and killed by members of the Front de Libération du Québec (FLQ) during the 1970 October Crisis.

▼ Sillery's Église Saint-Michel.
©Dreamstime.com/Andre Nantel

The **Maison des Jésuites de Sillery**, built of stone and covered with white plaster, occupies the former site of Saint-Joseph mission, of which a few ruins are still visible. In the 17th century, the mission included a wooden fence, a chapel and a priest's residence, as well as Aboriginal housing, a bakery, a brewery and a cemetery. As European illnesses such as smallpox and measles devastated the Aboriginal population, the mission was transformed into a hospice in 1702. At the same time, work began on the present house. In 1763, the house was rented to John Brookes and his wife, writer Frances Moore Brookes, who immortalized it by making it the setting for her novel *The History of Emily Montague*, published in London in 1769. It was also during this time that the structure was lowered and the windows were made smaller, in the New England saltbox tradition. The house now has two storeys in front and one in back, covered with a catslide roof.

By 1824 the main building was being used as a brewery and the chapel had been torn down. The house was later converted into an office complex for various shipyards. In 1929, the Maison des Jésuites became one of the first three buildings designated as historic by the government of Québec. Since 1948, it has housed a museum detailing the rich history of the property.

Domaine Cataraqui is the best-kept property of its kind still in existence in Sillery. It includes a large neoclassical residence, designed in 1851 by architect Henry Staveley, a winter garden and numerous outbuildings scattered across a beautiful garden. The house was built for a wood merchant named Henry Burstall, whose business operated at the bottom of the cliff on which the house stands. In 1935, Cataraqui became the

▲ Sillery's historic Maison des Jésuites.
©Dreamstime.com/Andre Nantel

▶ Discovering the sea bottom at the Parc Aquarium du Québec.
©Parc aquarium du Québec, Sépaq, Steve Deschênes

residence of painter Henry Percival Tudor-Hart and his wife Catherine Rhodes. They sold the property to the Québec government in 1975 to prevent it from being subdivided, as many others had been.

From the cliff to the river, the whole length of Boulevard Champlain between Côte de Sillery and Route de l'Église borders the **Promenade Samuel-De Champlain**. This 2.5km-long promenade aims to give the waterfront back to the people, with vast green spaces, a bicycle path and walking trails for everyone to enjoy. The park is divided into three sections—the Station des Cageux, the Station des Sports and the Station des Quais—hosting numerous recreational and sporting activities.

SAINTE-FOY

Maison Hamel-Bruneau is a beautiful example of British colonial architecture from the beginning of the 19th century. This style is characterized by hip roofs with flared eaves covering low wrap-

around verandas. Graced with French windows, Maison Hamel-Bruneau has been carefully restored and transformed into a cultural centre.

Formerly known as the "Aquarium du Pont de Québec", the magnificent **Parc Aquarium du Québec** was founded in 1959. Since then, it has welcomed over eight million visitors. Now home to over 3,500 fish species, the Parc Aquarium du Québec features over 16ha of ecosystems of the St. Lawrence River and the Arctic. When you first walk in, you can view a multimedia presentation that plunges you (virtually, of course) into the river and carries you to the North Pole.

Outside, you can follow the tours to meet various mammal species. You can also walk through a rocky valley along the shores of the St. Lawrence in a natural decor. Another must-see is the exhibit of the polar world of the

North. The polar bears and harp seals in this reconstituted Arctic never fail to impress. In the main building, you are transported from the marine universe of the Laurentian Plateau to the waters of the North Atlantic.

You can also visit the aquarium's laboratories and a huge circular basin known as the Grand Océan, in which you are surrounded by 350,000 litres of water inhabited by 650 marine specimens. You can even watch feedings and handle small invertebrates, such as starfish and sea urchins. The Parc Aquarium du Québec features rest areas, play areas for children, food services (the restaurant features a panoramic terrace offering a view of the St. Lawrence River and the bridges), as well as two souvenir shops.

The **Université Laval campus** extends south of Chemin Sainte-Foy and west of Avenue Myrand, a small but lively street

Sainte-Foy

and a favoured student haunt. Université Laval was founded in 1852, making it the oldest French-speaking university in America. It was first established in the heart of the old city near the seminary and Catholic cathedral before being moved to its current site 100 years later. The university was named in honour of Monseigneur de Laval, the first bishop of New France. Each year this vast campus welcomes some 40,000 students. It features good examples of modern and postmodern Québec architecture.

One of the more interesting buildings is the **PEPS** (sports and physical education building), built in 1971 near the corner of Chemin Sainte-Foy and Avenue du Séminaire.

A little further, **Pavillon Louis-Jacques-Casault** closes off the symmetrical perspective of the campus. This building was constructed from 1954-1958 according to the designs of Ernest Cormier, who also created the Université de Montréal's main building. In the beginning, Pavillon Louis-Jacques-Casault was to be the "Great Seminary" for priests in training, which explains the presence of a central chapel adorned with medieval-inspired towers. However, with the approach of the *Révolution Tranquille*

(Quiet Revolution), such a building was considered a dinosaur, reflecting the architecture of the past despite its recent construction. Since 1978, it has housed the faculty of music and the archive facilities of **Bibliothèque et Archives Nationales du Québec (BAnQ)**. The nearby **Pavillon J.A.-De Sève** and **Pavillon La Laurentienne** are clearly more modern.

At the Centre d'Accueil et de Renseignements de l'Université Laval, visitors can obtain information on campus activities. Finally, west of Avenue des Sciences-Humaines on Avenue de la Médecine in the Adrien-Pouliot pavilion is the **Musée de Géologie René-Bureau**, exhibiting fossils and minerals from around the world.

One of the most interesting gardens in Québec City is found on the university campus. **Jardin Botanique Roger-Van den Hende** is named after the Université Laval scientist who created it from scratch. Used for research and teaching, the garden is also open to visitors. The arboretum, herbaceous plant garden, rose garden and water garden are all worth a visit. Guided tours are also offered.

▼   Along Promenade Samuel De-Champlain. ©Gilbert Bochenek

▲ The monument in Parc des Braves. ©Mariette Provencher

THE BATTLE OF SAINTE-FOY

On April 27, 1760, the Chevalier de Lévis arrived from Montréal with 3,800 men and tried to capture Québec City, which had fallen to the British Army the previous autumn. Although they failed to enter the city, they succeeded in defeating General Murray's troops in Sainte-Foy, making this battle one of the only French victories of the Seven Years' War in New France. The name of the **Parc des Braves**, on Chemin Sainte-Foy, pays tribute to the courage of the valiant young men who made this bold move while waiting for help from a fleet of French reinforcements that would never arrive. In 1855, a monument designed by Charles Baillairgé was erected in their memory in the park. The statue of Bellona, a Roman war goddess, standing atop a cast-iron column, was a gift from Prince Jérôme-Napoléon Bonaparte. In 1930, landscape architect Frederick Todd redesigned Parc des Braves, attracting wealthy families from the old city to the park's surrounding area. The park has lovely views of the Basse-Ville and the Laurentian mountains.

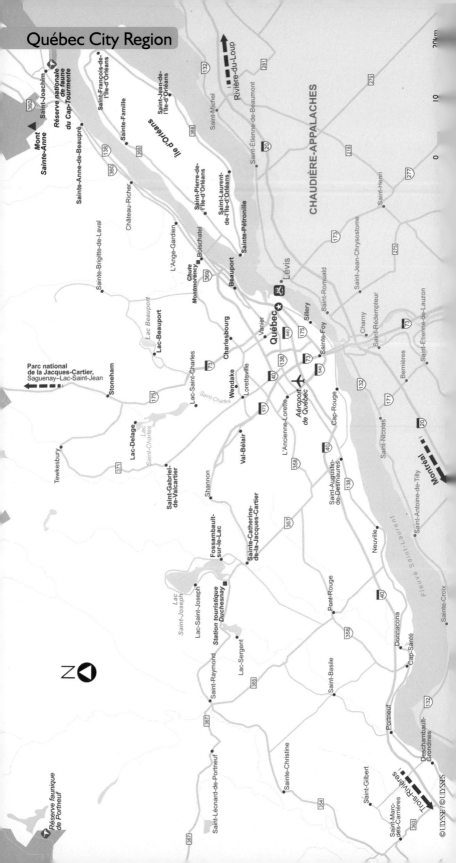

Québec City Region

North of the City

The area north of Québec City is crossed by several highways, whose first stop is Charlesbourg, one of the first areas to be populated in New France. From there, Route 369 leads to Wendake, a village inhabited by Canada's only Huron-Wendat community. The same road then leads west to Sainte-Catherine-de-la-Jacques-Cartier. Otherwise, from Charlesbourg, Route 73 heads to Lac Beauport, Lac Delage and Stoneham. Route 175 heads even further north, to Parc National de la Jacques-Cartier. As you may already have noticed, this entire region is a paradise for those who love the great outdoors.

▼ Charlesbourg's Moulin des Jésuites. ©Jean-Claude Germain

▲ Pretty Église Saint-Charles-Borromée, in Charlesbourg. ©Conseil du patrimoine religieux du Québec, 2003

North of the City

In New France, seigneuries were usually long rectangles marked out in squares that ran up and down hillsides. Most of them were set up perpendicular to a significant waterway as well. **Charlesbourg** is the only real exception to this system, but what an exception! In 1665, while looking for different ways to populate the colony and assure its prosperity and security, the Jesuits developed an original plan to urbanize their land: the Notre-Dame-des-Anges seigneury. It is a huge square that was divided into angled plots of land converging towards the centre where the dwellings were situated. The houses faced a square defined by a road called the Trait-Carré, where there was a church, a cemetery and a community pasture.

This concentric plan provided better defence against the Iroquois and is still visible today in the old part of Charlesbourg. Two other initiatives of this kind, Bourg Royal to the east and Petite Auvergne to the south, did not have the same success, however, and little remains of them today.

The Notre-Dame-des-Anges seigneury was granted to the Jesuits in 1626, making it one of the first permanent settlements inhabited by Europeans in Canada. Despite this early settlement and original seigneurial design, few buildings built before the 19th century remain in Charlesbourg. The fragility of the early buildings and the push to modernize are possible explanations.

Église Saint-Charles-Borromée revolutionized the art of building in rural Québec. Architect Thomas Baillairgé, influenced by the Palladian movement, was particularly innovative in arranging the windows and doors of the facade, to which he added a large pediment. Construction of the church began in 1828 and the original design has remained intact since. The magnificent interior decor by Baillairgé was done in 1833.

At the back of the choir, narrower than the nave, is the Arc de Triomphe-style retable, and in the centre is the tabernacle, evoking St. Peter's Basilica in Rome. A 17th-century painting by Pierre Mignard entitled *Saint Charles Borromée distribuant la communion aux pestiférés de Milan* (St. Charles Borromée giving communion to plague victims in Milan) also hangs there. Two beautiful statues by Pierre-Noël Levasseur, dating from 1742, complete the ensemble. When you step out, you can see the huge Second Empire-style 1876 presbytery, testament to the village priest's privileged status in the 19th century, and the Bibliothèque Municipale (municipal library) in the former Collège Saint-Charles (1904).

Maison Éphraïm-Bédard is one of the rare remaining houses in old Charlesbourg. The local historical society has occupied it since 1986 and presents an exhibition on the evolution of the Trait-Carré. Old maps and aerial photographs show the unique physical layout of Charlesbourg. Guided tours of the area are offered as well.

On Rue du Trait-Carré Est, you can see **Maison Magella-Paradis** at number 7970. Built in 1833, it occasionally hosts exhibitions. A little farther along at number 7985, **Maison Pierre-Lefevbre**, built in 1846, houses the **Galerie d'Art du Trait-Carré**. Works by various artists are featured here.

▲   Discovering Huron-Wendat handicrafts in Wendake. ©Jean-Claude Germain

The **Moulin des Jésuites,** a pretty roughcast rubble stone mill, is the oldest building in Charlesbourg. It was built in 1740 by the Jesuits, who were the landowners at the time. After several decades of neglect, the two-storey building was converted into the **Centre d'Interprétation de l'Histoire du Trait-Carré** and a tourist bureau in 1993. Concerts and exhibits are also presented here.

Lac Beauport is a resort site that is popular throughout the year. A downhill-skiing resort, Le Relais, has been created here. Around the lake, summer visitors can enjoy lovely beaches.

North of the City

Route 73 becomes Route 175 and runs through the resort towns of Lac-Delage and Stoneham, which is home to another ski resort. A bit further, the highway provides access to the Parc National de la Jacques-Cartier and the Réserve Faunique des Laurentides.

Forced off their land by the Iroquois in the 17th century, 300 Huron families moved to various places around Québec before settling in 1700 in Jeune-Lorette, today known as **Wendake**. Visitors will be charmed by the winding roads of this village, located on the banks of the Rivière Saint-Charles. The village's gift shop and museums, particularly the **Hôtel-Musée**

Premières Nations, provide a lot of information on the culture of this peaceful and sedentary people.

The **Église Notre-Dame-de-Lorette**, the Huron-Wendat church completed in 1730, is reminiscent of the first churches of New France. This humble building with a white plaster facade conceals unexpected treasures in its chancel and sacristy. Some of the objects on display were given to the Huron-Wendat community by the Jesuits, and come from the first chapel in Ancienne-Lorette (late 17th century). Among the works are several statues by Pierre-Noël Levasseur created between 1730 and 1740, an altar face depicting an Aboriginal village by Huron-Wendat

▼ Lac Beauport and its Catholic chapel. *©Rachid Lamzah*

sculptor François Vincent (1790) and a beautiful *Vierge à l'enfant* (Madonna and Child) sculpture by a Parisian goldsmith (1717). In addition, the church features a reliquary made in 1676, chasubles from the 18th century and various liturgical objects by Paul Manis (1715). However, the most interesting element is the small, Louis XIII-style gilded tabernacle on the high altar sculpted by Levasseur in 1722. The Tsawenhohi House offers guided tours.

Onhoüa Chetek8e is a replica of a Huron-Wendat village from the early colonial period. The traditional design includes wooden longhouses and fences. Visitors are given an introduction to the lifestyle and social organization of the ancient Huron-Wendat nation.

Maison Tsawenhohi bears the Huron-Wendat name of Grand Chief Nicolas Vincent, meaning "the one who sees clearly, the falcon." Built for him between 1807 and 1820, it is now part of the Huron-Wendat nation's heritage and houses an interpretation centre on traditional customs and a craft shop where you can watch artisans at work. Moose hair, porcupine quills, leather and birch bark are used to make baskets, moccasins, snowshoes and "water drums." In summer, guide services offer tours of the village's historic area.

▼ The Parc de la Falaise et de la Chute Kabir Kouba. ©*Parc de la Falaise et de la chute Kabir Kouba*

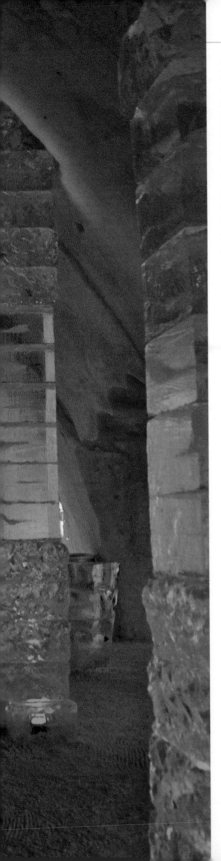

At the **Parc de la Falaise et de la Chute Kabir Kouba**, footpaths run along a 40m cliff above the Rivière Saint-Charles. A stairway leads to the magnificent 28m-tall Kabir Kouba waterfall. The site was long used for various types of mills (flour, lumber, paper) and a hydroelectric plant. The area is sacred to the Hurons, who consider the waterfall and river to be protectors of their nation. The **Centre d'Interprétation Kabir Kouba** is on the other side of the river in Loretteville. It recounts the history of the site through fossils, photographs and artifacts found nearby.

Sainte-Catherine-de-la-Jacques-Cartier is the gateway to the **Station Touristique Duchesnay**, a lovely park that, come wintertime, features the famous **Ice Hotel**. The Ice Hotel, a spectacular, Swedish-inspired structure, is unique in North America and definitely one of the region's "hottest" attractions. Its lifespan is obviously limited (early January to late March), but every year, builders return to the site to erect this stunning complex using several tonnes of ice and snow. And not only is the ice used for building, it also serves as decoration! The hotel houses an art gallery showcasing unusual snow and ice sculptures, as well as an exhibit room, a small movie theatre, a chapel and a bar where vodka is served in ice glasses.

◀   The Ice Hotel. ©Joyce Li

North of the City

Côte-de-Beaupré

This long, narrow strip of land nestled between the St. Lawrence River and the undeveloped wilderness of the Laurentian massif is the ancestral home of many families whose roots go back to the beginning of the colony. It illustrates how the spread of the population was limited to the riverside in many regions of Québec, and recalls the fragility of development in New France. From Beauport to Saint-Joachim, the colony's first road, the Chemin du Roy (king's road) built under orders from Monseigneur de Laval during the 17th century, follows the Beaupré shore. Along this road, houses are built in a style characterized by a raised stucco-walled main floor, long balconies with intricately carved wood balusters and lace-curtained windows.

Montmorency Falls. ©Shutterstock.com/André Nantel

▲   Montmorency Falls in winter. ©André Maurice

◀   Manoir Montmorency, nestled in Parc de la
Chute-Montmorency. ©Kristin C. Anderson

surgeon from the old Perche province of France. During the next few years he enthusiastically set about building a manor house, a mill and a small village, establishing one of the largest seigneuries in New France. Unfortunately, wars and fires have claimed several of these buildings.

The large white house known as **Manoir Montmorency** was built in 1780 for British governor John Haldimand. At the end of the 18th century, the house became famous as the residence of the Duke of Kent, son of George III and father of Queen Victoria. The manor, which once housed a hotel, was severely damaged by fire in May 1993. It has been restored according to the original plans and now features an information centre, a few shops and the Gril-Terrasse which offers an exceptional view of Montmorency Falls, the St. Lawrence River and Île d'Orléans. The small Sainte-Marie chapel on the property and the gardens are open to the public.

The Manoir Montmorency is nestled in the **Parc de la Chute-Montmorency**, created to preserve the magnificent spectacle of Montmorency Falls. Rivière Montmorency flows peacefully with its source in the Laurentians until it reaches a sudden 83m drop and tumbles into the void, creating one of the most impressive natural phenomena in Québec. One and a half times the height of Niagara Falls, **Montmorency Falls** flows at a rate that can reach 125,000 litres per second during spring thaw.

Visitors can take in this magnificent spectacle by following the pretty cliff path (Promenade de la Falaise) which passes by the Baronne lookout. The path also leads to two bridges, the Pont Au-dessus de la Chute and the Pont Au-dessus de la Faille, which cross the falls and the fault respectively and offer spectacular views. Picnic tables and a playground can be

Three types of urban development have shaped **Beauport** over the course of its history. Originally an agricultural settlement, in the 19th century it became an important industrial town, evolving into one of Québec City's main suburbs in the 1960s before merging with the city in 2002. In 1634, the Beauport seigneury from which the present city grew was granted to Robert Giffard, a doctor and

Côte-de-Beaupré

found in the eastern part of the park. The bottom of the falls can be reached via a 487-step panoramic staircase or a trail.

A cable car provides a relaxing and picturesque way to get back to the top. During winter, mist freezes into ice cones called "sugar-loaves" that adventurous souls can climb.

Samuel de Champlain, the founder of Québec City, was impressed by the falls and named them after the viceroy of New France, Henri II, duc de Montmorency. During the 19th century, the falls became a fashionable leisure area for the well-to-do of the region who would arrive in horse-drawn carriages or sleighs.

Château-Richer is charming and picturesque, highlighted by the striking situation of its church on a promontory. Hundred-year-old root cellars and stone ovens are visible from the road and are still used occasionally. Throughout the village, small wooden signs have been posted in front of historical buildings, indicating any distinctive architectural features and when they were built.

The superb **Moulin du Petit Pré**, which dominates the river of the same name on the edge of Chemin Royal, organizes tours with guides in period costumes. The windmill was rebuilt after the Conquest, modeled after the windmill that had been built by the Séminaire de Québec in 1695. It is the oldest wheat windmill in North America, and visitors can get a glimpse of the milling process. Since the late 1990s, beautiful vines grow behind the windmill. Inside, a shop sells regional products and flour that has been milled on-site.

The **Centre d'Interprétation de la Côte-de-Beaupré**, which used to be housed in the Petit-Pré windmill, was moved to a new location in the heart of the village. Now occupying a four-storey former school, the centre features a permanent exhibit on the history and geography of Côte-de-Beaupré, as well as temporary exhibits.

The interesting little **Musée de l'Abeille** offers a brief look into the lives of these tireless workers. Visitors can stroll through at their leisure or receive an introduction to the art of beekeeping by participating in a "bee safari." A beekeeper explains the steps involved in making honey and mead (honey wine). There is also a pastry shop and gift shop.

The long, narrow town of **Sainte-Anne-de-Beaupré** is one of the largest pilgrimage sites in North America. In 1658, the first Catholic church on the site was dedicated to Saint Anne after sailors from Brittany, who had prayed to the Virgin Mary's mother, were saved from drowning during a storm on the St. Lawrence River. Soon, a great number of pilgrims began to visit the church. The second church, built in 1676, was replaced in 1872 by a huge temple, which was destroyed by fire in 1922. Finally, work began on the present basilica which stands at the centre of a compound of chapels, monasteries and facilities as varied as they are unusual. Each year, Sainte-Anne-de-Beaupré welcomes more than a million pilgrims, who stay in the hotels and visit the countless souvenir boutiques, along Avenue Royale.

The **Basilique Sainte-Anne-de-Beaupré**, towering over the small, metal-roofed wooden houses that line the winding road, is surprising not only for its impressive size but also for the feverish activity it inspires all summer long. The church's granite exterior, whose colour varies with the light, was designed in the French Romanesque Revival style by Parisian

▲ An old home in Château Richer.
©Jean-Claude Germain

architect Maxime Roisin, assisted by Quebecer Louis Napoléon Audet. Its spires rise 91m high, while the nave is 129m long and the transepts over 60m wide.

The basilica's interior is divided into five naves, supported by heavy columns with highly sculpted capitals (by Émile Brunet and Maurice Lord). The vault of the main nave is adorned with sparkling mosaics designed by French artists Jean Gaudin and Auguste Labouret, recounting the life of Saint Anne. In a beautiful reliquary in the background, visitors can admire the Great Relic, supposedly a part of Saint Anne's forearm sent over from the Basilica of San Paolo Fuori le Mura in Rome. Finally, follow the ambulatory

▲ Detail of the facade of the Basilique Sainte-Anne-de-Beaupré. ©Marie-France Denis

around the choir to see the ten radiant chapels built in the 1930s, whose polychromatic architecture is inspired by the Art Deco movement. The basilica is open all year.

Materials retrieved after the demolition of the original church in 1676 were used to build the **Chapelle Commémorative** in

Côte-de-Beaupré

1878. The steeple (1696) was designed by Claude Baillif, an architect whose numerous other projects in 17th-century New France have all but disappeared because of war and fire. Inside, the high altar comes from the original church built under the French regime. It is the work of Jacques Leblond dit Latour (1700). The chapel is adorned with paintings from the 18th century. The water from the Fontaine de Sainte-Anne, at the foot of the chapel, is said to have healing powers.

The **Scala Santa**, an unusual yellow-and-white wooden building (1891), covers a staircase which pilgrims climb on their knees while reciting prayers. It is a replica of the Scala Santa, the sacred staircase conserved in Rome at San Giovanni in Laterano, said to be the one Christ climbed to get to the court of Pontius Pilate in Jerusalem. An image of the Holy Land is inlaid in each riser.

The **Chemin de la Croix** which extends behind the Chapelle Commémorative is located on the hillside. Its life-size statues were cast in bronze at Bar-le-Duc, France.

The **Cyclorama de Jérusalem**, a kitschy round building with Oriental features, houses a 360° panorama of Jerusalem on the day of the Crucifixion. This immense *trompe l'œil* painting, measuring 14m by 100m, was created in Chicago around 1880 by French artist Paul Philippoteaux and his assistants. A specialist in panoramas, Philippoteaux produced a work of remarkable realism. It was first exhibited in Montréal before being moved to Sainte-Anne-de-Beaupré at the very end of the 19th century. Very few panoramas and cycloramas, so popular at the turn of the century, have survived to the present day.

The **Musée de Sainte Anne** is dedicated to sacred art honouring the mother of the Virgin Mary. These interestingly diverse pieces were acquired over many years from the basilica and are now put on display for the public. Sculptures, paintings, mosaics, stained-glass windows and gold works are dedicated to the cult of Saint Anne, as are written works expressing prayers or thanks for favours obtained. The history of the pilgrimages to Sainte-Anne-de-Beaupré is also explained. The exhibition is attractively presented and spread over two floors.

To learn more about Québec folklore, go to the **Atelier Paré**. All the works presented at this wood-sculpting museum are inspired by the fascinating world of local legends.

▼　The Scala Santa. ©Andrew Belding

◀　The colossal interior of the Basilique Sainte-Anne-de-Beaupré. ©Thierry Ducharme

Île d'Orléans

Spanning some 32km by 5km, Île d'Orléans is an island set in the middle of the St. Lawrence River, downstream from Québec City.,It offers superb countryside, as well as some of the province's most cherished heritage treasures along historic Chemin Royal.

Of all Québec's regions, Île d'Orléans is the most evocative of life in New France. When Jacques Cartier arrived in 1535, the island was covered in wild vines which inspired its first name, Île Bacchus. However, it was soon renamed in honour of the Duc d'Orléans. All of the parishes on the island except Sainte-Pétronille were established during the 17th century. The colonization of the entire island followed soon after. In 1970, the government of Québec declared Île d'Orléans a historic district. The move was made in part to curb development that threatened to turn the island into just another suburb of Québec City, and also as part of a widespread movement among the Québécois to protect the roots of their French ancestry by preserving old churches and houses. Since 1936, the island has been linked to the mainland by a suspension bridge, the Pont de l'Île. Île d'Orléans is also known as the country of Félix Leclerc (1914-1988), the most famous Québec poet and *chansonnier*.

This tour around Île d'Orléans will allow you to enjoy its many charms: its old buildings dating from the French Regime, the small chapels that line the road, the large fields that seem to plunge into the river, the orchards, and more. Depending on the season, you may also be able to pick fruit. Don't be surprised if, along the way, you see penned llamas or ostriches. Barely 10 years ago, this island only had old-fashioned black and white cows, but today, new kinds of farming have developed, greatly increasing what you can see here.

Paradoxically, **Sainte-Pétronille** is both the site of the first French settlement on Île d'Orléans and also its most recent parish. In 1648, François de Chavigny de Berchereau and his wife Éléonore de Grandmaison established a farm and a Huron-Wendat mission here. However, constant Iroquois attacks forced the colonists to move further east to a spot facing Sainte-Anne-de-Beaupré. It was not until the middle of the 19th century that Sainte-Pétronille was incorporated as a village, as its beautiful location began attracting numerous summer visitors. Anglophone merchants from Québec City built beautiful second homes here, many of which are still standing along the road. Sainte-Pétronille's wharf dates back to 1855 and offers a magnificent view of Québec City.

During her life, Éléonore de Grandmaison had four husbands. After the death of François de Chavigny, she

▼ Manoir Gourdeau. ©Yves Laframboise

married Jacques Gourdeau who gave his name to the estate, his wife's property. Overlooking the river from the top of a promontory, **Manoir Gourdeau**, on Chemin du Bout-de-l'Île, has been given this name even though the house's construction date does not quite coincide with the time the couple was together. The long building was most likely built at the end of the 17th century but has been considerably expanded and changed since then.

Rue Horatio-Walker is named after **Maison Horatio-Walker**. The red brick building and the stucco house beside it were respectively the workshop and residence of painter Horatio Walker from 1904 to 1938. The British-born artist liked the French culture and meditative calm of Île d'Orléans. His workshop, designed by Harry Staveley, remains a good example of English Arts and Crafts architecture.

The Porteous family, of English origin, settled in Québec City at the end of the 18th century. In 1900, they built the **Domaine Porteous**. This vast country house surrounded by superb gardens was christened "La Groisardière." Designed by Toronto architects Darling and Pearson, the house revived certain aspects of traditional Québec architecture. The most notable of these is the Louis XV-inspired woodwork and the general proportions of the house, similar to the Manoir Mauvide-Genest in Saint-Jean. Inside are

numerous paintings by William Brymner and Maurice Cullen depicting countryside scenes on Île d'Orléans. The building also incorporates Art Nouveau features. The property, which today belongs to the Foyer de Charité Notre-Dame-d'Orléans, a seniors' residence, was expanded between 1961 and 1964 when a new wing and a chapel were added.

Until 1950, the main industry of **Saint-Laurent-de-l'Île-d'Orléans** was the manufacturing of *chaloupes* (barges), boats and sailboats that were popular in the United States and Europe. Though production of these boats has ceased, some traces of the industry, such as abandoned boatyards, can still be seen off the road near the river bank. The village was founded in 1679 and still has some of its older buildings, such as the beautiful **Maison Gendreau**, built in 1720 on Chemin Royal, west of the village, and the **Moulin Gosselin**, also on Chemin Royal but east of the village, which now houses a restaurant.

The **Parc Maritime de Saint-Laurent** has been developed on the site of the Saint-Laurent shipyard. Here you can visit the Godbout *chalouperie* workshop, a family business established around 1840. They have a collection of nearly 200 craftsmen's tools. A path behind the building leads to the water.

▼ The Parc Maritime de Saint-Laurent.
©Parc Maritime de Saint-Laurent

▼ Along the shore in Saint-Jean-de-l'Île-d'Orléans. ©Annie Caya

In the mid-19th century, **Saint-Jean-de-l'Île-d'Orléans** was the preferred home base of nautical pilots who made their living guiding ships through the difficult waters and rocks of the St. Lawrence River. Some of their neoclassical and Second Empire houses can still be seen along Chemin Royal and provide evidence of the privileged place that was held by these seamen, who were indispensable to the success of commercial navigation.

The most impressive remaining manor from the French Regime is in Saint-Jean. The **Manoir Mauvide-Genest** was built in 1734 for Jean Mauvide, the Royal Surgeon, and his wife, Marie-Anne Genest. This beautiful stone building has a rendering coat of white roughcast in the traditional Norman architectural style. Now an interpretation centre on the New France seigneurial system, the manor also houses a renowned French restaurant, the Restaurant du Manoir.

Saint-François-de-l'Île-d'Orléans, the smallest village on Île d'Orléans, retains many buildings from its past. Some, however, are far from the Chemin Royal and are difficult to see from the road. The surrounding countryside is charming and offers several pleasant panoramic views of the river, Charlevoix and the coast. The famous wild vines that gave the island its first French name, Île Bacchus, can also be found in Saint-François.

Just outside the village is an observation tower which provides excellent views to the north and east. Visible are Île Madame and Île Au Ruau, which mark the point where the St. Lawrence River's fresh and salt waters meet. Mont Sainte-Anne's ski slopes, Charlevoix on the north shore and the Côte-du-Sud seigneuries on the south shore can also be seen in the distance.

▲ The Parc des Bisons de l'Île d'Orléans.
©Jeff Hawkins

▶ Manoir Mauvide Genest.
©Jean-Pierre Garceau Bussières

The **Parc des Bisons de l'Île d'Orléans** is a unique concept that allows you to observe the magnificent bison up close. In both a natural setting (three lakes outfitted for canoeing, kayaking, pedal-boating and inflatable rafts) and a ranch (120ha pasture), the Parc des Bisons features the largest bison herd in Québec, with over 400 animals. You can then explore the park (along a 4km dirt road with interpretation panels on the edge of the lakes) in your own vehicle

or take the footpath (45min return trek, accessible to wheelchairs) that leads to an elevated site where you can admire a panoramic view of the surroundings (Mont Sainte-Anne, Cap Tourmente, the Côte-du-Sud and the bison park). The park's restaurant, Le Bison Futé, serves excellent bison meat-based meals. All in all, the park provides a total change of scenery, right on the island.

The oldest parish on Île d'Orléans, **Sainte-Famille** was founded by Monseigneur de Laval in 1666, in order to establish a settlement across the river from Sainte-Anne-de-Beaupré for colonists who had previously settled around Sainte-Pétronille. Sainte-Famille has retained many buildings from the French Regime. Among them is the town's famous church, one of the greatest accomplishments of religious architecture in New France and the oldest two-towered church in Québec.

The beautiful **Église Sainte-Famille** was built between 1743 and 1747 to replace the original church built in 1669. Although its facade was framed by two towers, its single bell tower, unusually, was located on the roof ridge. In the 19th century, the two towers gave way to two new steeples, bringing the total number of steeples to three and making the church one of a kind in Québec.

Although modified several times, the interior decor retains many interesting elements. Sainte-Famille was a wealthy parish in the 18th century, thus allowing the decoration of the church to begin as soon as the frame of the building was finished. In 1748, Gabriel Gosselin installed the first pulpit, and in 1749 Pierre-Noël Levasseur completed the construction of the high altar's present tabernacle. Louis-Basile David, inspired by the Quévillon school, designed the beautiful coffered vault in 1812. Many paintings adorn the

church, such as *La Sainte Famille* (The Holy Family), painted by Frère Luc during his stay in Canada in 1670, the *Dévotion au Sacré Coeur de Jésus* (Devotion to the Sacred Heart of Jesus, 1766) and *Le Christ en Croix* (Christ on the Cross), by François Baillairgé (1802). The church grounds offer a beautiful view of the coast.

Most of the French Regime farmhouses on Île d'Orléans were built a good distance from the road. Today these properties are much sought after and their owners guard their privacy jealously, which makes any visiting unlikely. Fortunately, a foundation has been set up by residents so that **Maison Drouin** is open every summer to visitors. It is one of the oldest houses on the island and in Québec, dating from around 1675 and enlarged in 1725. Built from large fieldstones and wooden beams, it was inhabited until 1984 and was never modernized. You will learn about its history from guides dressed in period costumes acting out the daily life of its former inhabitants. The three rooms on the ground floor, as well as the upstairs, recall the environment of the first colonists. Antique furniture and tools are also displayed to help illustrate pioneer life, making it a lovely place to visit.

Saint-Pierre-de-l'Île-d'Orléans, the most developed and populated parish on Île d'Orléans, had already lost some of its charm before the island was declared a historic site. Saint-Pierre is particularly important to the people of Québec, since it was the home of renowned poet and singer Félix Leclerc (1914-1988) for many years. The singer and songwriter who penned "Le P'tit bonheur" was the first musician to introduce Québécois music to Europe. He is buried in the local cemetery.

At the end of the village is a site honouring the poet's memory. The **Espace Félix-Leclerc** includes a wide array of

◀ Église Sainte-Famille and its three steeples.
©Annie Caya

FÉLIX LECLERC, QUÉBEC'S GREAT TROUBADOUR

Félix Leclerc, one of Québec's greatest singer-songwriters and poets, was born on August 2, 1914 in La Tuque in the Mauricie region, the sixth of 11 children.

Beginning his career on the radio, he was ever afterwards a man of language. His songs, stories, poems and plays express the world and its people as nobody else's could.

He lived part of his life in Paris, where he performed his songs such as "Le P'tit bonheur" and "Moi mes souliers" on the greatest stages of the capital. Besides singing, he published poetry (*Calepin d'un flâneur*, *Chansons pour tes yeux*), plays (*Qui est le père?*, *Dialogues d'hommes et de bêtes*), short stories (*Adagio, Allegro, Andante*) and novels (*Le fou de l'île*, *Pieds nus dans l'aube*). He won numerous international awards.

He founded theatre companies, put together radio dramas, played, recorded, published, performed on stage, and above all, knew how to move his listeners.

Only in December 1969 did he finally purchase land on Île d'Orléans, which he had made famous in his songs and stories. When he returned to Québec, he built a house in Saint-Pierre on the island and moved in with his family. The island had captured his heart from his first summer visit in 1946, and he paid it back by exploring it and drawing inspiration from it. In his song "Le tour de l'île," he sang: "This island is like Chartres, tall and clean, with naves, arches, aisles, and cliffs."

Félix Leclerc lived in Saint-Pierre for nearly 20 years. When he died on August 8, 1988, with his wife, daughter, and son at his side, he left them and all Quebecers a cultural inheritance beyond measure. Today, the Espace Félix-Leclerc, a museum, cultural centre, and green space in the village of Saint-Pierre, keeps the poet's memory alive.

▶ The Espace Félix Leclerc. ©Philippe Renault/Hemis

interesting features: a building housing an exhibit on the life and work of Félix Leclerc, a boîte à chansons (music venue for singer-songwriters) where young and old alike can belt out Leclerc's famous tunes or come up with some new ones of their own, and hiking trails to explore the heart of the island.

Église Saint-Pierre, a humble but lovely building erected in 1716, is the oldest village church still standing in Canada. The church is also a rare survivor of this kind of architecture, which was widespread in New France. It only has one portal and an oculus window on the facade. Most of these little churches with pointed roofs were destroyed in the 19th century and replaced with more elaborate structures. Pillaged during the Conquest, the interior of Église Saint-Pierre was rebuilt at the end of the 18th century. Note the altars by Pierre Émond (1795), embellished with the papal coat of arms. The paintings above the altars are by François Baillairgé.

This church was abandoned in 1955 when the larger nearby church was inaugurated. However, when it was threatened with demolition, it was taken over by the Québec government. Conserved intact, it displays furnishings no longer found in most Québec churches, such as a central stove with a long iron stovepipe. The pews have doors which allowed these closed spaces to be reserved as private property; in winter, the owners kept warm with hot bricks and furs. This little church is worth the trip, even if only to encourage Quebecers to watch over their heritage and be proud of it.

Île d'Orléans

Major Themes

Seasons in Québec

Québec's seasonal extremes set the province apart from much of the world. Temperatures can rise above 30°C in summer and drop to -25°C in winter. Visiting Québec during the two "main" seasons (summer and winter) is like having visited two totally different countries, with the seasons influencing not only the scenery, but the lifestyles and behaviour of the province's residents.

Winter

"Mon pays ce n'est pas un pays, c'est l'hiver..."

("My country is not a country, it's winter")

– Gilles Vigneault

Mid-November to the end of March is the best time for skiing, snowmobiling, skating, snowshoeing and other winter sports. In general, there are five or six large snow storms per winter. Howling wind often makes the temperatures bitterly cold, causing "drifting snow" (very fine snow that is blown by the wind). One bright spot is that though it may be freezing, Québec gets more hours of winter sunshine than Europe.

Spring

Spring is short, lasting roughly from the end of March to the end of May, and heralded by the arrival of "slush," a mixture of melted snow and mud. As the snow disappears, plants and grass, yellowed by frost and mud, come to life again. Nature's welcomed reawakening is spectacular.

Summer

Summer in Québec blossoms from the end of May to the end of August and may surprise some outsiders who think of Québec as a land of snow. The heat can be quite extreme and often seems much hotter because of the accompanying humidity. The vegetation becomes lush, and don't be surprised to see some rather exotic red and green peppers growing in window boxes. The streets of Québec City are decorated with flowers, and restaurant terraces are always full. The season also sees many different festivals.

Fall

The fall colours can last from September to November. Maple trees form one of the most beautiful living pictures on the North American continent as their leaves are transformed into a kaleidoscope of colours from bright green to scarlet to golden yellow. Temperatures will stay warm for a while, especially during what is commonly called "Indian Summer," but eventually the days and especially the nights will become quite cold.

Indian Summer

This relatively short period (only a few days) during the late fall is like summer's triumphant swan song. Caused by warm air currents from the Gulf of Mexico, this phenomenon is called Indian Summer because it represented the last hunt before winter. Aboriginals took advantage of the warm weather to stock up on provisions before the cold weather arrived.

▸ Parc National de la Jacques-Cartier and its snaking river.
©Parc national de la Jacques-Cartier, Sépaq, Mathieu Dupuis

◂ Québec as seen from the south shore of the St. Lawrence River. © Rachid Lamzah

Seasons in Québec

▲ A thrilling ride down the Rivière Jacques-Cartier. ©*Parc national de la Jacques-Cartier, Sépaq, Mathieu Dupuis*

Summer Activities

Bird-Watching

One of the best places in the region for bird-watching is the Cap-Tourmente National Wildlife Area in Saint-Joachim. In spring and autumn, the thousands of migrating snow geese that overtake the area are a fascinating sight to behold. Any questions you might have after seeing these creatures up close and in such great numbers can be answered here. The reserve is home to 280 species of birds, attracted here throughout the year by a number of bird houses and feeders.

Cruises

Croisières AML organizes cruises all summer, offering a great view of Québec City and its surroundings from a different angle. One of the ships owned by this company is the *Louis-Jolliet*, which sails from Québec City, its port of registry. Day cruises go as far as Montmorency Falls. At night, you can go up to Île d'Orléans and enjoy dinner in one of the ship's two dining rooms. These evening cruises feature musicians and dancing.

From Québec City, Croisières Groupe Dufour takes passengers to the lovely Charlevoix region, Pointe-au-Pic, Île-aux-Coudres and even to the heart of the breathtaking Saguenay fjord, among other destinations.

▲ Snow geese over the Cap-Tourmente National Wildlife Area. ©istockphoto.com/Marcel Pelletier

Cycling

Québec City is developing its cycling infrastructure. Today, more than 100km of cycling paths stretch out around the city and its surroundings. Among others, a bike path called the Corridor des Cheminots enables cyclists and other sports enthusiasts to travel 22km through various municipalities to Val-Bélair.

Some noteworthy bike paths have existed for a number of years, such as the one that leads to Beauport or the one that runs along Rivière Saint-Charles. The many separate or shared routes make Québec City and its neighbouring communities enjoyable places to discover by bicycle.

The Promo-Vélo association offers a great deal of information on the various kinds of tours available in the region, and publishes a map of bike paths in the Québec City region.

A bicycle path runs from the Vieux-Port of Québec City to the Parc de la Chute-Montmorency, passing through Beauport on the way. Also, roads such as the Chemin du Roy and those on the Côte de Beaupré and Île d'Orléans, are meant to be shared by motorists and cyclists. Caution is always in order, but these trips are definitely worth the effort.

Following the route of some old railway lines, the Piste Jacques-Cartier–Portneuf crosses through the Réserve Faunique Portneuf and the Station Touristique Duchesnay (where you can park your car and rent bicycles), and borders a number of lakes. It stretches 68km from Rivière-à-Pierre to Saint-Gabriel-de-Valcartier. Its magical setting and safe riding conditions attract many cyclists. In winter, the path is used for snowmobiling.

Summer Activities

Fruit-Picking

From strawberries and raspberries to corn, leeks and apples, the harvests follow one another all summer long, continuously changing the look of the surrounding countryside. On Île d'Orléans, farmers open their doors to anyone, parents and children alike, who wishes to spend a day playing in an orchard or a field. Learn the secrets of picking and enjoy the fruits of your labour!

Golf

The Royal Charlesbourg is an 18-hole golf course located far from the hustle and bustle of the city. The Mont-Tourbillon 18-hole golf course is a great place to enjoy this sport. Station Touristique Mont-Sainte-Anne's golf course, Le Grand Vallon, is a par 72 course with several sand traps and four lakes, and is known as one of the most interesting courses in eastern Canada.

Hiking

The 100km of paths in Parc National de la Jacques-Cartier, near Lac-Beauport, are among the best for hikers in this region. Whether gentle or rugged, they will allow you to discover the hidden corners of the forest, as well as superb views of the valley and the river.

At the Cap-Tourmente National Wildlife Area, if your legs are up to it, you can climb the 20km of trails that lead to a magnificent view of the river and its sur-roundings. You can also use the board-walks (adapted for people with dis-abilities) for an equally enjoyable walk.

◀ Hiking in the forest of Station Touristique Duchesnay.
©Station touristique Duchesnay, Sépaq, Steve Deschênes

▼   In-line skating on the Plains of Abraham.
     ©Philippe Renault/Hemis

▼   Mont-Sainte-Anne's ski trails welcome
     mountain bikers in summer.
     ©istockphoto.com/Gaby Jalbert

Near Beaupré, Station Touristique Mont-Sainte-Anne has 32km of hiking trails.

In-Line Skating

On the Plains of Abraham in front of the Musée National des Beaux-Arts du Québec is a large paved rink perfect for in-line skating. Scores of helmeted children and adults can be seen blading around the track on fine summer days. Equipment rentals are available at a small stand by the rink. This is the only spot on the Plains of Abraham where blading is allowed.

Jogging

Again, the place to go is the Plains of Abraham. The big flat track in front of the Musée National des Beaux-Arts

du Québec is a good place for a run, though people also go jogging on the paved lanes and trails.

Mountain-Biking

Near Beaupré, Station Touristique Mont-Sainte-Anne has about 200km of trails to offer mountain-bike enthusiasts. Pedal your way to the top of the mountain on the downhill skiing trails or rush down the slopes after riding up in the cable car with your bicycle. There are more than 20 trails with most evocative names, such as La Grisante (the exhilarating one) or La Vietnam. This is a well-known biking spot: World Cup Mountain Bike races are held here every year. Bike rentals are available on site.

Parc National de la Jacques-Cartier, near Lac-Beauport, is also popular among mountain bike enthusiasts.

Summer Activities

Rafting

In spring and summer, the Rivière Jacques-Cartier gives adventurers a good run for their money. Two longstanding companies offer well-supervised rafting expeditions with all the necessary equipment. At Village Vacances Valcartier, in Saint-Gabriel-de-Valcartier, an 8km ride delivers a lot of excitement. Tubing is also available. With Excursions Jacques-Cartier, in Tewkesbury, you can also experience some very exciting runs.

Waterslides

The Village Vacances Valcartier outdoor activity centre in Saint-Gabriel-de-Valcartier is the undisputed authority when it comes to slides. The waterslides and wave pools draw big crowds. A restaurant and bar can be found on site, and a vast 700-site campground is available.

Winter Activities

Cross-Country Skiing

The snow-covered Plains of Abraham provide an enchanting setting for cross-country skiing. Trails crisscross the park from one end to the other, threading their way through the trees or leading across a headland with views of the icy river. All this right in the heart of the city!

Some extremely pleasant cross-country ski trails can also be found at Domaine Maizerets in Limoilou. At the starting point, there is a little heated chalet with a wood-burning stove. Equipment rentals are available.

Station Touristique Duchesnay, in Sainte-Catherine-de-la-Jacques-Cartier, is very popular among skiers in the area. This great forest boasts 57.5km of well-kept cross-country ski trails (as well as 12.5km of skate ski trails) and hosts tiny chickadees and other bird species that don't mind the cold!

Nestled in the heart of the Réserve Faunique des Laurentides, Camp Mercier is criss-crossed by 190km of well-maintained trails in an extremely tranquil landscape. Given its ideal location, you can ski here from autumn to spring. Long routes (up to 42km) with heated huts offer some interesting opportunities. There are also cottages for rent that can accommodate two to 14 people.

Summer Activities

▲   Sliding on Terrasse Dufferin. *©Philippe Renault/Hemis*

The Station Touristique Mont-Sainte-Anne, near Beaupré, has 300km of well-maintained cross-country ski trails with some heated huts set up along the way. The Sports Alpins ski shop on Rang Saint-Julien, in Saint-Ferréol-les-Neiges, rents the necessary equipment.

Downhill Skiing and Snowboarding

Le Relais, in Lac-Beauport, has 27 downhill skiing trails, all of which are lit for night skiing. The Station Touristique Stoneham has 32 runs, 17 of which are lit at night. Station Touristique Mont-Sainte-Anne, near Beauport, is one of the biggest ski resorts in Québec. Among its 63 runs, some reach 625m in

▲   Place D'Youville becomes a skating rink in winter. *©Philippe Renault/Hemis*

height and 15 are lit for night skiing. It's equally a delight for snowboarders.

Le Massif, in Petite-Rivière-Saint-François, is one of the best ski resorts in Québec. Firstly because it features the highest vertical drop in eastern Canada (770m), and secondly, because of the heavy snow of every winter, which, aided by artificial snow, creates ideal ski conditions. Then there's the amazing natural setting! The mountain, which almost plunges into the river, offers a stunning panorama. There are 45 runs for all types of skiers, and a cozy chalet awaits you at the summit.

Ice Skating

Each winter, an ice rink is laid out on Terrasse Dufferin, enabling skaters to twirl about at the foot of Château Frontenac with a view of the icy river. You can don your gear at the kiosk.

On beautiful winter days, Place d'Youville becomes a magical place, with skaters, snow, frost-covered Porte-Saint-Jean, the illuminated Capitole and Christmas decorations hanging from lampposts. In the centre of the square is a skating rink with music, and even if you don't feel like joining in the ice waltz, you can still enjoy the sights. Thanks to its cooling system, the skating rink opens early in the season, around the end of

▼ Le Massif, in Petite-Rivière-Saint-François, one of the area's best ski resorts. ©Marc Archambault

October, and shuts down in late spring, ensuring that Québec City residents can skate for as long as possible! There are dressing rooms (bring a padlock) with washrooms for skaters.

A lovely skating rink winds beneath the trees of Domaine Maizerets in Limoilou. There's a small chalet nearby where you can take off your skates and warm up next to a wood stove. Skate rentals are available.

Once it has iced over, the Rivière Saint-Charles is turned into a natural skating rink that, weather permitting, winds 2km between the neighbourhoods of Limoilou and Saint-Roch, in Basse-Ville. There is a heated place to rest and skates can be rented on site.

Snowshoeing

Snowshoeing, a sport that regained its popularity when smaller, lighter models of snowshoes began to appear on the market, can be practised in most of the region's cross-country skiing centres. The Station Touristique Duchesnay, the Station Touristique Mont-Sainte-Anne, as well as Parc National de la Jacques-Cartier near Beauport, are some of the nicer snowshoeing sites.

Tobogganing

During winter, a tobogganing slope is created on Terrasse Dufferin. First purchase your tickets at the little stand in the middle of the terrace, then grab a toboggan and climb to the top of the slide. Once you get there, make sure you take a look around: the view is magnificent!

The hills of the Plains of Abraham are wonderful for sledding. Bundle up and follow the kids pulling toboggans to find the best spots!

The undisputed biggest name in ice slides is Village Vacances Valcartier in Saint-Gabriel-de-Valcartier, an outdoor resort with everything ice sliders need to have a good time. Ice slides will help you forget the cold for a little while. There is also snow rafting and skating on a 2.5km-long ice rink that snakes through the woods. Restaurant and bar on site.

Natural Sites

With its big trees and lawns, Domaine Maizerets is the perfect place for a leisurely stroll. Gardening buffs will love the arboretum and the landscaping; the Domaine also belongs to the Association des Jardins du Québec. In the heart of the arboretum is a butterfly aviary. Weather permitting (closed when it rains), visitors can walk into this world of butterflies, which features some 30 species from eastern Canada. The sight will amaze you, and you can learn about the different stages of their development. All sorts of outdoor activities can be enjoyed here in both summer and winter. Outdoor concerts, plays and talks on ornithology and other subjects are held at the Domaine Maizerets all year round.

In Beaupré, the Canyon Sainte-Anne is where the rushing Rivière Sainte-Anne carves a deep path through the hills near Beaupré and plunges 74m into a large 22m pothole formed by the resulting current. Visitors can take in this impressive sight from lookouts and a suspension bridge.

Cartier-Brébeuf National Historic Site is a small park on the banks of Rivière Saint-Charles. It has been redesigned as a pleasant spot for people to enjoy a stroll. Freed from its concrete walls, at least in this area, the river is adorned with aquatic plants. Flowers and decorative trees also embellish the park.

Battlefields Park, better known as the Plains of Abraham, is Québec City's undisputed king of parks. This immense green space covers some 100ha and stretches all the way to Cap Diamant, which slopes down to the river. It is a magnificent place for local residents to enjoy all sorts of outdoor activities. Strollers and picnickers abound during the summer, but there is more than enough space for everyone to enjoy a little peace and quiet.

Throughout the year, hordes of visitors come to Parc National de la Jacques-Cartier, located in the Réserve Faunique des Laurentides near Lac-Beauport, 40km north of Quebec City. The area is called Vallée de la Jacques-Cartier, after the river that runs through it, winding between steep hills. As a result of the microclimate caused by the river being hemmed in on both sides, the site offers a number of outdoor activities. The vegetation and wildlife are abundant

▲ The butterfly aviary at Domaine Maizerets. ©Société du Domaine de Maizerets

▶ The impressive Canyon Sainte-Anne. ©Canyon Sainte-Anne

and diverse. The winding and well-laid-out paths sometimes lead to interesting surprises, such as moose and their offspring foraging in a marsh. Before heading out to discover all the riches the site has to offer, you can get information at the nature centre's reception area. Campsites chalets and equipment are all available for rent. At the park, specialists organize moose observation safaris as well as a sunset Rabaska canoe animal-watching tour, introducing visitors to the animals in their natural habitat.

On the shores of the river, at the limits of what used to be the towns of Sainte-Foy and Cap-Rouge, Parc de la Plage-Jacques-Cartier allows residents to fully enjoy the St. Lawrence River. There didn't use to be many places to stroll leisurely along the riverbanks and admire the water, the tides, the birds and the boats, but today, this beach allows everyone to appreciate the majesty of this important source of life.

On the shores of Lac Saint-Joseph, near the village of Fossambault-sur-le-Lac, stretches the Plage Lac Saint-Joseph. You're not dreaming: this is a real tropical beach, complete with palm trees—imported from Florida annually! In addition to swimming, you can enjoy a wide array of water activities here. Note, however, that the beach attracts a large crowd on hot summer days.

The Cap-Tourmente National Wildlife Area is located on fertile pastoral land. Each spring and autumn, its sandbars are visited by countless snow geese that stop to gather strength during their long migration. The reserve also has bird-watching facilities and naturalists on hand to answer your questions about the 280-odd species of birds and 45 species of mammals you might encounter on the hiking and walking trails that cross the park.

Near Beaupré, Station Touristique Mont-Sainte-Anne covers 77km² and includes the 800m-high Mont Sainte-Anne, one of the most beautiful downhill ski sites in Québec. There are a few hotels close to the ski hill and the park. Various other activities are also offered, since the park has 200km of mountain-bike and cross-country ski trails. Sports equipment can be rented on site.

About 45km from Québec City, on the shores of the region's largest lake, Lac Saint-Joseph, the Station Touristique Duchesnay in Sainte-Catherine-de-la-Jacques-Cartier introduces visitors to the Laurentian forest. Long famous for its cross-country ski trails, it is also ideal for all kinds of outdoor activities, such as hiking on its 25.7km network of maintained footpaths, 15km of which are part of the Trans-Québec hiking path. There are also ample opportunities for water sports. The Jacques-Cartier–Portneuf bike path also crosses Duchesnay. In addition, an interpretation pavilion hosts various educational and awareness-raising activities. The installations offer comfortable lodging and dining. In winter, the site is home to the Ice Hotel.

▼   The Cap-Tourmente National Wildlife Area. ©Philippe Renault/Hemis

Art and Culture

Québec City has always enjoyed a very impressive and varied cultural life. The city is home to numerous artistic and cultural centres, including the Grand Théâtre de Québec (which hosts the Orchestre Symphonique and the Opéra de la Capitale), the Palais Montcalm, the Théâtre du Trident, the Théâtre de la Bordée, the Théâtre du Périscope and the Théâtre du Conservatoire d'Art Dramatique de Québec.

During the 19th century, Québec City was the setting of many novels. Although the most popular genre at the time was European-style adventure stories, Québec literature was usually limited to glorifying the past and idealizing country life, and was clearly behind the times when compared to Western literature in general. In the beginning, the use of Québec City as a setting was hardly recognizable but became increasingly evident over the years. As more novels were published, from *Les Anciens Canadiens* by Philippe Aubert de Gaspé to Roger Lemelin's well known *Au pied de la pente douce* (1944) and *Les Plouffe* (1948), Québec City's image changed from that of a vague, undefined place to a very lively, bustling French Canadian city. Even though it was once conquered by the British and is not as commercially significant as other cities, Québec remains the intellectual capital of French Canada and a symbol of resistance for French Canadians.

Roger Lemelin (1919-1994), a successful writer who described the colourful poor neighbourhoods of Québec City in his novels *Au pied de la pente douce*, *Les Plouffe* and *Le Crime d'Ovide Plouffe* (1982), was born in Québec City. These last two works became very popular and were adapted for radio and television, then for the movies. In 1974, Lemelin was elected as a foreign member of France's Académie Goncourt.

Famed novelist Anne Hébert (1916-2000) was born in Sainte-Catherine-de-la-Jacques-Cartier, in the Québec City region. Her novel *L'Enfant chargé de songes* (1992) brings the city to life as though it were an actual character.

Several contemporary writers also originate from this region, such as mystery writer Chrystine Brouillet, novelists Yves Thériault, Monique Proulx and Marie-Claire Blais and poet Pierre Morency.

Numerous artists such as Cornelius Krieghoff, Maurice Cullen, James Wilson Morrice, Clarence Gagnon, Adrien Hébert, Jean-Paul Lemieux, Jean-Guy Desrosiers and others have been influenced by this city and at the same time have enriched its image.

▼ Québec City's Grand Théâtre. ©Louise Leblanc

Art and Culture

▲ Roger Lemelin (1919-1992).
   ©Archives Nationales du Québec

▲ Félix Leclerc (1914-1988). © Michel Elliot, P404, 9
   mars 1972 (Photos F. Leclerc)/Archives nationales du Québec - M

Art and Culture

Several artists have found inspiration in the region and have chosen to settle in Québec City or the surrounding region. For example, Félix Leclerc (1914-1988), a composer, poet and performer, was the first Québec singer to achieve success in Europe, opening the way for many other Québec artists. Leclerc spent his free time on Île d'Orléans, a place that was close to his heart and that is featured prominently in his work.

Today, Québec City continues to be a birthplace for interesting artistic projects. Performing-arts centres such as Méduse and Ex Machina are just two examples in a city where theatres and other artistic institutions abound. Québec's film industry is also quite rich. Among the city's rising stars is Francis Leclerc, son of Félix Leclerc, and creator of the beautiful film *Une jeune fille à la fenêtre*, in which images of Québec City bear witness to the filmmaker's affection for his hometown.

Ex Machina was founded by Robert Lepage in 1994. Born in the Haute-Ville section of Québec City on December 12, 1957, this director and producer has enjoyed a remarkable international success. Not unlike Félix Leclerc, it took his huge popularity in Europe to make Québec recognize Lepage's immense talent. This skill is particularly evident in his plays *Les Plaques Tectoniques*, *La Trilogie des dragons* and *Les Aiguilles et l'opium* as well as his films *Le Confessionnal*, *Le Polygraphe*, *Nô*, *Possible Worlds* and *La Face cachée de la lune*. From opera to theatre and cinema to rock concerts and major events (his *Image Mill* presented during the festivities surrounding Québec City's 400th anniversary was the world's largest multimedia show), Robert Lepage has done it all.

▲   *The Image Mill*, by Robert Lepage. ©Nicolas Franck Vachon

The Carnaval de Québec in winter, the Festival d'Été de Québec in summer, the Fêtes de la Nouvelle-France, the world beats of the Festival des Journées d'Afrique and the Festival Interculturel de Québec, all in August, delight residents and tourists alike with days of extravagant celebration.

Architecture

Québec City is first and foremost the only walled city on the North American continent north of Mexico. The city was fortified for security reasons and its position on top of Cap Diamant was strategic. Champlain had Fort Saint-Louis built at the beginning of the 17th century.

Originally, the walls served to defend against British threats and ward off Aboriginal attacks. Very early on, major fortification work transformed Québec City into a veritable stronghold: the city saw the construction of the Batterie Royale in 1691, the Dauphine Redoubt in 1712, and in 1720, the walls that more or less make up the ramparts we see today. The buildings inside the walls and in Vieux-Québec give the city its Old French Regime look.

Québec City has one of the richest architectural heritages in North America. As the cradle of New France, it is especially evocative of Europe in its architecture and atmosphere. But its architecture had to be adapted to the harsh winters and lack of specialized workers and materials in the colony. The buildings here are simple and efficient without extravagance. A typical house of this period was rectangular in shape with a two-sided sloping roof covered with

Architecture

cedar shingles. To cope with the cold Québec City winters, this type of habitation was fitted with only a few windows and one or two fireplaces. Interiors were quite rustic, since the main preoccupation was to keep warm at all times.

Although this type of dwelling was found mainly in the countryside, the same kind of architecture could also be seen within the city itself. As well as having to deal with the cold, the city's inhabitants had to worry about fires. The proximity of the buildings and their wooden construction meant that fires could spread very quickly. Following the great fire of 1682, which almost completely destroyed the Basse-Ville, the intendants of New France issued two edicts in 1721 and 1727 regulating construction in order to reduce the risk of fire inside the city walls. From then on, the use of wood and the construction of mansard roofs—their structure was complex and compact, presenting a great danger for fire—were both prohibited. All buildings had to be made of stone and equipped with firewalls. In addition, the floors that separated a house's storeys had to be covered with terra cotta tiles.

In neighbourhoods such as Petit-Champlain you will find stone houses dating from this era, such as the Maison Louis-Jolliet at on Rue du Petit-Champlain or the Maison Demers on Boulevard Champlain. The decision to forbid the use of wood also resulted in the creation of the first suburbs outside city walls, since the poorer settlers were unable to meet the costly building requirements and were forced to move out of town.

Following the British victory on the Plains of Abraham, New France became part of the British Empire and the face of Québec City gradually changed as its anglophone population increased. For instance, on Grande Allée, once a simple, tree-lined country road, large estates appeared where the English built Second Empire and, later on, Victorian mansions. Today, these buildings have been transformed into bars or restaurants with terraces overlooking Grande Allée.

Among the city's large-scale projects is the revitalization of the Saint-Roch district, the once neglected and unloved downtown core. Since work started

▲ One of Grande Allée's old mansions, now
transformed into a bar and restaurant.
©Philippe Renault/Hemis

in 1990 in partnership with numerous
organizations, the district has welcomed the Université Laval's École
des Arts Visuels and the Méduse arts
centre, while residents and businesses
have returned in force. Other renova-
tion projects have targeted the Place de
la Gare, the surroundings of the Hôtel
du Parlement, Boulevard René-Lévesque
and Avenue Honoré-Mercier.

◄ Charming European-style terraces.
©Istockphoto.com.com/Tony Tremblay

▶ Stone houses in the Petit-Champlain
neighbourhood. ©Istockphoto.com.com/Tony Tremblay

Index

Contact Information

Offices

Canada: Ulysses Travel Guides, 4176 St. Denis Street, Montréal, Québec, H2W 2M5, ☎514-843-9447, ▤514-843-9448, info@ulysses.ca, www.ulyssesguides.com
Europe: Les Guides de Voyage Ulysse SARL, 127 Rue Amelot, 75011 Paris, France, ☎01 43 38 89 50, voyage@ulysse.ca, www.ulyssesguides.com

Distributors

U.S.A.: Hunter Publishing, 130 Campus Drive, Edison, NJ 08818, ☎800-255-0343, ▤732-417-1744 or 0482, comments@hunterpublishing.com, www.hunterpublishing.com
Canada: Ulysses Travel Guides, 4176 St. Denis Street, Montréal, Québec, H2W 2M5, ☎514-843-9882, ext. 2232, ▤514-843-9448, info@ulysses.ca, www.ulyssesguides.com
Great Britain and Ireland: Roundhouse Publishing, Millstone, Limers Lane, Northam, North Devon, EX39 2RG, ☎1 202 66 54 32, ▤1 202 66 62 19, roundhouse.group@ukgateway.net
Other countries: Ulysses Travel Guides, 4176 St. Denis Street, Montréal, Québec, H2W 2M5, ☎514-843-9882, ext.2232, ▤514-843-9448, info@ulysses.ca, www.ulyssesguides.com